GOLD RUSH COUNTRY

By the Editors of *Sunset Books* and *Sunset Magazine*

LANE BOOKS · MENLO PARK, CALIFORNIA

HOURS, ADMISSION FEES, AND PRICES IN THE EDITORIAL CONTENT OF THIS BOOK ARE AS OF JANUARY 1972.

Research and Text: Barbara Braasch
Supervising Editor: Elizabeth Hogan

Cartography: Roberta A. Perez-Dillow
Topographical Maps: Jack Doonan

Front cover: Firemen are polishing an elegant old hand-pumper Papeéte, which arrived in Columbia in 1859. Columbia is preserved as a state historic park, and, through the restoration of old buildings, park officials are recreating a mining town representative of the time between 1850 and 1870. Front and back covers photographed by Glenn Christiansen.

Executive Editor, Sunset Books: David E. Clark

Third Printing September 1973

FOREWORD

The event that first focused on California the rapt attention of the rest of the world was, of course, Jim Marshall's finding of a few flakes of yellow metal in the tailrace of Captain Sutter's new sawmill beside the American River. What happened during the next half-dozen years forms one of the most dramatic chapters in the nation's history. For a horde of argonauts, traveling by land and water, converged on California from all points of the compass, and in their ardent hunt for gold explored every nook and cranny of the Sierra foothills from Madera County northward to Mount Shasta and beyond.

During their brief stay in the Mother Lode country, the gold hunters left an impress on the land that more than a century has failed to erase. To be sure, during the hundred years that have elapsed since then, many changes have occurred. Some of the once populous early-day camps have disappeared entirely; the sites of others are marked only by heaps of rubble and a few ruined walls, while yet others have become prosperous towns, their streets lined with substantial modern buildings of brick or stone.

With this fine book on the arm of his comfortable chair or the seat of his moving car, the reader can better "travel through" the exciting past of the Gold Rush Country. It is in one volume a solid contribution to both Western travel literature and Californiana. For those who today venture into the area, whether by armchair or automobile, will find on its pages precisely that information, briefly and authentically set forth, that will enable them to understand and appreciate the abundance of historical lore that still clings to virtually every stream, every town, and every abandoned campsite. Without some such mentor, much of the romance of the region would surely be missed; with it, it becomes easy to seek out those relics of the past that enable one to visualize the stirring events which took place there a century or more ago.

Incidentally, it is altogether appropriate that this excellent guidebook to the Mother Lode country should have been compiled and issued by the publishers of *Sunset* Magazine. For *Sunset*, since its founding three-quarters of a century ago, has devoted itself to chronicling the attractions of life in the West, and although it has been mainly concerned with the contemporary scene, from time to time it has turned backward to reveal to present-day readers some phase of the region's eventful past.

Oscar Lewis

ACKNOWLEDGMENTS

Ever-increasing interest and inevitable changes in the Gold Country have resulted in four editions of this book since it was first published in March, 1957. Dozens of writers and editors have contributed to the previous editions, and we are especially appreciative of the efforts of William Bronson and Robert Iacopi.

Special thanks for help in preparing this fourth edition go to Cecil Helms, who shared his knowledge of the area with us; architect Ted Moulton, who explained Gold Country architecture; the California Department of Parks and Recreation; Candi Ancker of Auburn; Ivan Branson of Rough and Ready; Kenneth M. Castro of Murphys; Carlo DeFerrari of Sonora; John Hassler of Coloma; William S. Murphy of Los Angeles; Oliver P. Stewart of Grass Valley; Ray S. Thompson of Auburn; Dr. R. Coke Wood of Murphys; Maud Lindemann, Madera County Historical Society; Joan Faust, Mariposa County Historical Society; Patricia H. Rhodes, Tuolumne County Historical Society; W. P. Fuller, Jr., Calaveras County Historical Society; Clyde R. Berriman, Amador County Historical Society; Dr. Paul L. Washburn, El Dorado County Historical Society; Jim Oliver, Tuolumne County Chamber of Commerce; Gertrude Waller, Calaveras County Chamber of Commerce; Carol Hughes, Hangtown Chamber of Commerce; Joy Woods, Auburn Area Chamber of Commerce; and all the other Chambers of Commerce throughout the Gold Country.

CONTENTS

SPECIAL FEATURES

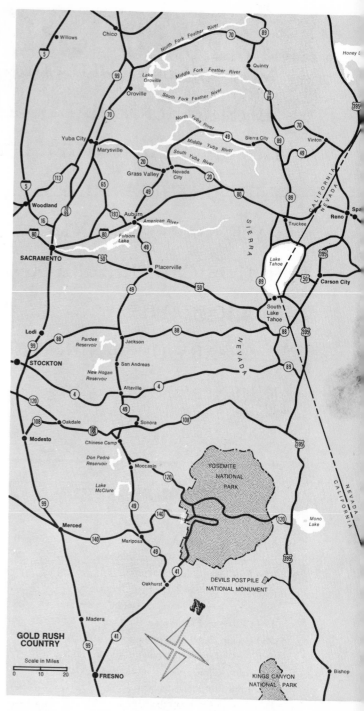

Stone houses *still stand as sentinels of the past throughout much of the Gold Country. You'll see them along State Highway 49 or on some of the side roads. Boy* **(left)** *is getting "leg up" to peer into house near Angels Camp. A rusted pot* **(right)** *rests on frame sill of house in Jackson Valley.*

INTRODUCING GOLD COUNTRY

WHAT IT IS
WHERE TO VISIT
WHEN TO GO

"**M**ONDAY 24TH this day some kind of mettle was found in the tail race that looks like goald first discovered by James Martial, the boss of the mill."

With this innocent and barely legible entry in his diary, Henry W. Bigler recorded the moment in January, 1848, that changed the course of Western history and set hearts palpitating throughout the world. Henry Bigler was a workman at Sutter's sawmill in the Sierra Nevada foothills, a virtually unexplored area in early 1848. Neither he nor James "Martial" realized that within a year the primitive territory of California would be known from Australia to Wales, and a great migration would begin that would open the West.

The fortune-seeking miners were called "Forty-niners," in respect to the first big year of the California Gold Rush; but there were also '48ers and '53ers and many more who responded to the lure of gold. The dream of quick and easy riches had universal appeal, and men drooled over the first stories that came out of California. Nuggets as big as your fists, just lying there on the ground to be picked up by passing strangers. Gravels so rich that a single panful could produce the fortune of a lifetime. Gold, as much as you wanted, waiting in the foothills of California.

The fact that mining in the Gold Country was miserable drudgery, filled with disappointments, does not seem to dull this glorious image. Those who worked knee-deep in icy water to dig out just enough gold to pay the astronomical prices of bed and board, or toiled long hours deep in a quartz mine, lost their naivete in a hurry. But the millions who learned about the Gold Rush only through hand-me-down legends will always carry with them the image of the big strike, the free ride for life.

It's true that miners once dug up a single gold nugget that weighed 195 pounds. However, during the early days, it was not unusual for a miner to pay a dollar for a slice of bread and another dollar to butter it. He paid $100 for a blanket, $100 for a horse, and $20 for a shovel with which to dig his fortune or his folly. The many who sought their living by the less exhausting route of supplying these miners with food, clothing, tools, transportation, and amusement were the ones who really "struck it rich."

A miner's tastes were simple. Most of his time was spent in grubbing in the ground for elusive gold. Relaxation generally came in the form of conversation, card playing, singing if there happened to be a fiddler around, or in playing practical jokes. Occasionally a traveling circus, a theatrical troupe, or bull and bear fights broke up the monotony.

If he desired more in the form of recreation, he had to journey to the nearest large settlement where there was always a saloon or fandango hall. Women were few and far between during those early days of the Gold Rush. At most dances you could only tell the "ladies" from the gentlemen by seeing which one had the handkerchief tied around his arm.

The California Gold Rush will always be remembered — not only for its great historical and economic importance but also for its unique character and its unique characters. Extremes were the order of the day during the Gold Rush, and there are literally hundreds of stories that will never cease to cause listeners to shake their heads in wonder and disbelief.

This disbelief is sometimes justified, since many stories have a way of getting bigger and better with each retelling. Yet for each tall tale, there are a dozen real anecdotes that do not need the added frills of exaggeration. Towns really did grow up overnight and disappear almost as fast.

Panning, picnicking, *and examining plaques— these may be memories you bring back after retracing the path of the argonauts. Man* **(above)** *is trying his luck at gold panning. Plaque dedicated to Marshall* **(bottom right)** *is at Coloma. Monument near Oakhurst* **(top right)** *marks beginning of Gold Rush Highway.*

One of the saddest aspects of the Gold Rush Country is that there is so little left — so few *things* — to go with the stories of that wild and crazy time. Many of the gold-mining camps were flimsy and temporary to begin with, and more than a hundred years of harsh weather and human neglect has taken its toll. The California Division of Mines and Geology estimates that 500 towns were born in the Gold Rush Country between 1848 and 1860. Far more than half of these settlements are completely gone. Of the remainder, a big percentage are little more than names on signposts. Only a handful managed to thrive after the gold was gone and adapt themselves to the changes of twentieth-century life.

CHANGE IS INEVITABLE

Even since the first edition of this book was published in 1957, there have been some notable changes in Gold Rush territory. A fire has taken a good many of Jamestown's handsomest old wooden buildings; a highway alignment has erased the last remains of Mormon Bar; the waters of the Merced River have drowned Bagby; a freeway has cut through Nevada City; Jacksonville has disappeared under the waters of the reservoir behind the Don Pedro Dam; and Robinson's Ferry will one day be inundated. Grass Valley's traffic congestion has been relieved by a freeway that destroyed some of the gold-mining sites; and the Auburn Dam, which will deepen and widen the American River, will take away even more of this area's colorful past.

More changes are inevitable: Who knows where the next fire will strike, or where the next "recreational area" will be planned, or what portion of the Mother Lode Highway must be realigned? Weather, too, works against the old adobe and stone structures. Buildings crumble a little more with each winter, until they finally collapse or are washed down to the foundations.

There are a few bright spots. Chambers of commerce and organized citizens' groups work mightily to save the old buildings and preserve at least some of the old-time atmosphere. Fortunately, there have been some notable successes. Private enterprise lends a helping hand on occasion; some of the new banks and other commercial buildings are being painstakingly constructed in the finest tradition of authentic Gold Rush architecture and make handsome additions to old mining towns.

MINERS' TEN COMMANDMENTS

Miners were forced to write their own laws which gradually spread throughout the camps and became known as the Miners' Ten Commandments. In 1853, they were enacted into Federal law. Here is a condensed version.

1. Thou shalt have no other claim than one.
2. Thou shalt not make any false claim nor jump one. If thou do thou must go prospecting and shall hire thy body out to make thy board and save thy bacon.
3. Thou shalt not go prospecting before thy claim gives out. Neither shall thy take thy gold to the gambling table in vain.
4. Thou shalt remember the Sabbath. Six days thou mayest dig, for in six days labor thou canst work enough to wear out thy body in two years.
5. Thou shalt not think more of thy gold than how thou shall enjoy it.
6. Thou shalt not kill thy body by working in the rain. Neither shall thou destroy thyself by getting "tight" nor "high seas over" while drinking down thy purse.
7. Thou shalt not grow discouraged, nor think of going home before thou hast made thy pile.
8. Thou shalt not steal a pick, a shovel or a pan from thy fellow miners, nor borrow a claim, nor pan out gold from others riffle box. They will hang thee, or brand thee like a horse thief with the letter R upon thy cheek.
9. Thou shalt not tell any false tales about "good diggings" in the mountains, lest your neighbors return with naught but a rifle and present thee with its contents thereof and thou shall fall down and die.
10. Thou shall not commit unsuitable matrimony nor neglect thy first love. If thy heart be free thou shall "pop the question" like a man, lest another more manly than thou art should step in before thee, and then your lot be that of a poor, despised comfortless bachelor.

The towns that have been by-passed by new highways are perhaps the most fortunate. Three of these — Jackson, Mokelumne Hill, and Jamestown — have managed to retain many of their false-fronted buildings. Antique shops have given new life to old buildings, and old hotels have been renovated to serve today's travelers. These towns still have the feeling of the frontier West.

Even more fortunate are places like Sheepranch or Fiddletown which are off the beaten path. They seem to doze quietly in the sun, untouched by progress.

HIGHWAY 49—
PATH TO ADVENTURE

This book covers the area on the western slopes of the Sierra Nevada between Oakhurst and Vinton that was the main mining center during the Gold Rush. This is by no means all of the gold-bearing land in California. There were rich diggings around Weaverville, in the Bodie area, and in the Southern California hills. But the Gold Rush Country considered here was the major gold belt and the scene of most of the action.

Fortunately for the traveler, the Gold Rush Country is traversed by a good highway, appropriately numbered State Highway 49 (although it is a county road from Oakhurst to the Mariposa County line) and designated by the State Legislature as the Mother Lode Highway.

You can see a good many of the major mining camps just by staying on this one highway. It's hard to resist the side roads, though, for it is here that you will find the little out-of-the-way towns that often reflect more of the Gold Rush atmosphere than the bigger towns along Highway 49. You will notice that many of the most historic mining camps mentioned in this book are on those intriguing side roads, some of which are clearly marked and easy to locate, others which may involve a little wandering — one of the pleasures of any trip to the Gold Country.

Not all of Highway 49 is picturesque. The outskirts of some of the larger towns, for example, were not planned for sightseers. But these brief passages are forgotten when you're on the country-lane stretch between Cool and Pilot Hill, or the spectacular switchbacks between Bear Valley and Coulterville. A portion of the highway in the Tahoe National Forest, Yuba County, was designated a scenic highway in 1971.

The Gold Country ranges in altitude from rolling grassland a few hundred feet above sea level to the 6,700-foot elevation of fir-clad, often snowy Yuba Pass. State Highway 49 stays at around 2,000 feet, except where it dips into the deep river canyons and where it climbs the mountains above Downieville. In summer, the weather is likely to be fiercely hot at the lower levels but much more pleasant in the pine belt. Dust will probably be deep on the unpaved logging roads and on the trees beside them, just as it was along the thoroughfares traveled by the coaches during the Gold Rush days.

When fall arrives, the first rains settle the dust and wash the oaks, poplars, locusts, and eastern maples in time for them to brighten the old towns with yellow and vermilion. In winter, rain turns the red foothill soil to mud and snow covers the higher altitudes. Touring can still be a pleasure, though, and many of the old ruins look better in the rain than they do under the heat of August.

At the lower elevations, spring comes along early in February and March. La Porte still may have some snow in April or May, but the rest of the foothills are green with new grass and colorfully dotted with wildflowers. As the days grow longer, you'll find mile after mile of blazing Scotch broom, and fields of lupine, owl's clover, Mariposa lily, buttercup, brodiaea, Mexican firebush, and the glorious California poppy.

WHEN TO PLAN A VISIT?

Every season has its advantages. Gold panning is best in the spring when the snow melts in the higher mountains filling dry stream beds. But if

Exploring *the Gold Country takes time. If you rush you might miss this art gallery at "Mok Hill"* **(top left),** *a tempting side road like the one near Ben Hur* **(bottom left),** *an architectural gem such as Mariposa's courthouse* **(top right),** *or the shady cemetery at Iowa Hill* **(bottom right).**

Sagging porch *of a once-proud home in Copperopolis should warn would-be explorers of possible danger.*

Line forms *outside the Claypipers theater at Drytown; troupe performs melodramas on summer weekends.*

you're planning on swimming in some of those deep rivers, better wait until the summer sun has had a chance to warm icy depths.

Summer (between Memorial Day and Labor Day) is, of course, the most popular tourist season. You will find the area heavily visited and overnight accommodations more difficult to obtain, but this is the time when theatrical groups will be performing and when most of the colorful local events take place. It's also wise to remember that the schedules of shops, museums, and other historical attractions are very erratic, and they are more likely to be open daily during the summer and on weekends in the spring and fall.

For spectacular wildflower displays, plan your trip in the spring. Flowers will first start their showing in the southern portion of the Mother Lode. The Gold Country seems very appropriately named in the fall as the leaves begin to change, providing brilliant splashes of color against the rolling golden hills.

Winter is the snow season and many ski resorts (for example, Bear Valley, Dodge Ridge) operate a few miles east of Highway 49. It's also a time when Christmas shopping is a pleasure. As you gaze into gaily decorated windows that display toys designed to delight the hearts of children a

century ago, you may feel you have stepped back into the pages of time. Inns with cozy fires, the scent of hot cider and freshly-cut pine boughs enhance the feeling.

BIG TOWNS, SMALL TOWNS, OR NONE AT ALL?

There is some dispute whether you'll find more of the Gold Rush atmosphere in the little deserted ghost towns or in the communities that still teem with activity. The decaying settlements have a timeless quality about them, and there is great charm in the old ruins, particularly if you can explore and photograph them when early-morning or late-afternoon light casts long shadows among the crumbling stone walls and rusty iron shutters.

On the other hand, the big towns like Sonora or Jackson or Grass Valley more closely resemble life in the Gold Rush days than do the sleepy ghost towns. The crowds that fill the shop-lined streets in these noisy, bustling communities are more like the lively crowds that thronged the camps in an earlier day. There may be little of picturesque quality left on the main streets, but of course there

Amador County Museum *building in Jackson was once the home of a local lawyer and politician. Today it contains many Gold Rush artifacts including a working model of the Kennedy Mine and a stamp mill.*

was probably nothing picturesque about the old town in the eyes of those who lived there a century ago. Some of the good-sized towns have two faces: the main street is busy and modern, but the side streets are still narrow and crooked and lined with old houses and stores that are closer to the Gold Rush than they are to the present day.

Don't forget to visit the sites of towns that are now only colorful names in history. Keep a sharp eye out for crumbling walls, scarred hillsides, tailings, rusting mining equipment, or an overgrown cemetery. Often these are the only remnants of a once boisterous, prosperous settlement. It's not hard to conjure up visions of former activity. Tombstones often tell terse stories of a prospector's unfilled dreams.

AVAILABLE INFORMATION

Data is dispensed generously and enthusiastically in this tradition-proud land. Chambers of commerce are very active, and you can obtain maps and printed guides just for the asking. Therefore, it's easy to become well informed on the Gold

Rush, and if authorities sometimes conflict on dates or the validity of one story or another, they generally agree on most things.

The California Division of Highways, local historical societies, the California Historical Landmarks Advisory Committee, E Clampus Vitus, and the Native Sons and Daughters of the Golden West have erected scores of markers throughout the countryside, and you can get a good idea about the area just by reading these alone. Museums — good ones — are almost everywhere and generally worth your time. There are also a number of gift stores and antique shops where you can buy authentic artifacts, second-hand junk, and even raw gold.

The Golden Chain Council of the Mother Lode, a citizens' organization with nine member counties, publishes a colorful map of the Gold Country with information on points of interest in each county. You can usually pick them up at the county chambers of commerce or by writing to the Council's headquarters in Murphys.

Most county historical societies publish quarterly bulletins with much factual data on the Mother Lode. Your public library can also provide a great deal of information, and the gold regions will mean much more after you've sampled some of

Use this book *as a guide to remainders of area's colorful past. Gaze at headframes of famous mines like the Central Eureka at Sutter Creek* **(top left)**; *detour to "almost" ghost towns of Copperopolis* **(bottom left)** *or Hornitos* **(top right)**; *or visit museums like one in Murphys* **(bottom right)**.

the absorbing literature that the land and its people have inspired. The stories of Mark Twain and Bret Harte are well-known. Some of the quietest rural landscapes come to rollicking life with Joseph Henry Jackson's *Anybody's Gold*. And winding down to nondescript Rich Bar after sampling the *Shirley Letters* is like going home. The selected reading list at the back of this book includes suggestions for obtaining additional information on different facets of the Gold Rush era.

Some of the relics require no literary build-up. It's enough, for instance, just to stand in the Mariposa County courthouse and know that it has remained virtually unchanged since the days when John C. Fremont fought many legal battles to hold on to his vast empire.

HOW TO USE THIS BOOK

The three main chapters of this book are based on an arbitrary division of the Gold Rush Country: Southern Mines, Central Mother Lode, and Northern Mines. Each section within these chapters centers around at least one major town where you will find accommodations. Each section would take at least a full weekend to cover if you plan to do anything more than merely drive through the old towns. But as convenient as the divisions are from this standpoint, there is no historical or geographical importance to the lines we have drawn, unless, of course, they happen to coincide with county lines, too.

This edition of the book contains a portion of Madera County for the first time. Although the mines in this region never attained the historical importance attributed to those farther north, much gold was taken out and many colorful characters wandered through the area.

On the opening pages of each chapter, you will find a road map that will help you locate the towns mentioned in the text. The towns are not discussed in any strict geographical order, but rather in the order you might encounter on a motoring trip driving from south to north. The routes followed are, of course, only representative of many you might want to plan. We have suggested several alternates in various sections.

Most of the roads mentioned are paved, although only a few stretches of Highway 49 could be regarded as a freeway. Some of the side trips involve driving over dirt roads, all passable during the summer. Remember that in the higher elevations of the northern Sierra, snow will often keep back roads closed well into the summer.

In looking at a map you may find a road which looks like a much closer connection between two towns than the route we have selected. There are various alternatives, but don't try them unless you're willing to backtrack if the road ends along the bank of a river.

In remote areas, always be sure to have plenty of gasoline and be prepared for an impromptu picnic. Gas stations, grocery stores, restaurants, and overnight accommodations may be few and far between when you venture far off the main highways. Yet it's these same back roads that lead to places little changed since they were glimpsed by the first argonauts.

You can probably drive the 310 twisting miles of Highway 49 between Oakhurst and Vinton in a day, but you won't see much. A long weekend will let you pause at the markers and absorb a smattering of lore, with little time out for picture-taking. You can make a pretty thorough reconnaissance of Highway 49 in a week, but you would need twice as much time to include the side trips without which some of the most meaningful places are missed. Perhaps the best way to see the Gold Country is simply to explore it section by section a few days at a time.

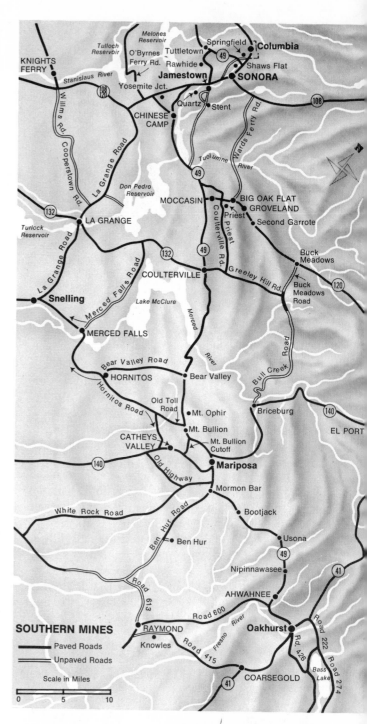

Map, above, *helps you locate the Gold Rush towns in the Southern Mines section. Some are on State Highway 49, others are on smaller side roads. Old wagon* (left) *is on display in a building at Hornitos, and the bearded prospector* (right) *is giving gold-panning instructions at Columbia.*

THE SOUTHERN MINES

OAKHURST · MARIPOSA
HORNITOS · CHINESE CAMP
SONORA · COLUMBIA

GOLD HAD been discovered in small quantities along rivers as far south as Madera County before the announcement of James Marshall's find farther north in 1848; however, it took a while for miners to leave the well-publicized areas and trickle down to the Southern Mines.

The placer and quartz veins in the Southern Mines never rivaled those to the north. This part of the country was better known to Mexican ranchers and Indian traders than any other section of the Gold Country. Spectacular scenery and the eventual discovery of Yosemite National Park brought tourists almost as soon as it did prospectors.

This area is still sparsely settled, and the section between Oakhurst and Mariposa has been virtually overlooked in most books dealing with California's gold discovery. But Oakhurst is the southern terminus of the Mother Lode Highway, and some of the surrounding mines were as famous as any in the Mother Lode.

OAKHURST AND NEARBY

Although there were once some 67 mines operating in the rich fields around Oakhurst, today there is little evidence of this once hectic activity. Besides decaying structures, remnants of mining days include a jail (part of a motel) in Oakhurst, a well pump at Coarsegold, and a stone fence along the Ben Hur Road.

You can explore this area on several different routes. You can simply drive Highway 49 from

Oakhurst to Mariposa, or you can take State Highway 41 south from Oakhurst to Coarsegold and follow back-country roads over to Raymond, returning to State 49 on County Road 600 or on the Ben Hur Road.

Oakhurst. First named Fresno Flats, Oakhurst was never a typical miner's town because there was little gold in the immediate vicinity. The nearest major mine was the Enterprise, about 5 miles downstream on the Fresno River. The first settlers, who began arriving in 1856 and 1857, demonstrated a keen interest in establishing a permanent community rather than a settlement that might last but a few months or years like many of the transient gold camps. A school was started, and the post office began operations in 1873.

Today's casual observer sees little of historic interest in the bustling little town, a tourist stop on the way to Yosemite National Park. However, two remnants of its more romantic past are found in town right on State Highway 41. The old jail that served Fresno Flats is now one of the units at the Holiday Village Motel. Refurbished inside, the exterior looks much as it might have in 1887. Some of the motel's other cabins were moved from Miami Lodge, an old stage stop between Ahwahnee and Yosemite. One is said to have been headquarters for Teddy Roosevelt during his tour of Yosemite in 1903.

The little frame Christ Church, built in Fresno Flats in 1891, stands about a block down the street from the present motel. It was moved to this knoll atop Oakhill Cemetery in 1957 and is now known as the "Little Church on the Hill." Buried in the cemetery is Lieutenant Skeens, an army officer killed in the first battle of the Mariposa Indian War which took place near Ahwahnee in 1851.

Around Oakhurst are many once-booming mining camps that have crumbled into dust and passed into oblivion; a few small communities survive but appear to have turned their backs on their turbulent past; some are just colorful names like String Town and Poison Switch.

Coarsegold. Eight miles south of Oakhurst on State 41 is one old mining town that still survives. Named for the texture of gold found in the area, Coarsegold became a thriving community overnight when miners began picking up gold nuggets from the creek beds. Although the city claimed a population of 10,000 inhabitants at one time, it is more likely that 1,500 miners swarmed over the hills in its heyday.

A single nugget worth $15,000 was the beginning of a mining claim called Texas Flats — one of the oldest and most extensively worked "hardrock" mines in the area. One story relates that four Texas latecomers were persuaded by some of the "old hands" to work a supposedly worthless hill mine. It proved to be quite rich, and the four quickly acquired a fortune before temporarily losing the vein. Another of its colorful owners was William (Bill) Henderson, among those who claimed to have killed Joaquin Murieta (see page 27). Most of the easy finds were over about 1890, but the Texas mine was worked until the 1900's, following the elusive vein to a depth of nearly 900 feet, one of the deepest of the Southern Mines. All that is left of this mine is rubble; the stamp mill burned in 1927.

Later, thousands of Chinese moved into the area and reworked old placer claims, patiently moving many tons of dirt and gravel, to be rewarded by little of value.

A surviving remnant of the past is an old pump that once serviced a well dug in the middle of the main street to furnish the town with water. It was surrounded by a wooden platform and covered with a tin roof. A cornerstone inscription, "1852," testifies to its many years of service.

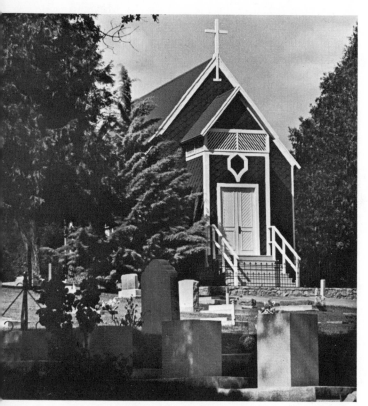

Frame church *standing on knoll in Oakhurst cemetery was built in 1891 when town was called Fresno Flats.*

Anyone wishing *to spend a night in jail is welcome at Holiday Village Motel in Oakhurst. The original jail of Fresno Flats has been remodeled inside, but the exterior looks like it did when built in 1887.*

Narbo. Although no longer in existence, this was the site of a short-lived "French Occupation." In 1883, a "salted" mine 3 miles south of Coarsegold was sold to a Frenchman named Marcellin Fache, a foolish tenderfoot. Fache formed a corporation called Quartz Mountain Mill Company by appealing for funds through the churches in France. An expensive water-powered 60-stamp mill was installed with little thought to the fact that this was an area singularly lacking in water. Using Chinese labor, a 25-mile ditch was dug to what is now known as Bass Lake before it was discovered water rights could not be obtained. Meanwhile, a lumber mill, bought for construction of flumes and mine buildings, proved useless when no water was available.

Without water, the wheel wouldn't turn and the mill wouldn't run. In sheer desperation, the reckless owners invested another $15,000 in a marine motor. After many delays, the mill machinery was set in motion. However, the stamp-mill operator, having been told one pound of quicksilver (which trapped fine gold) would be necessary to catch $1,000 worth of gold, obviously figured if one pound was good, 100 pounds was better. His theory proved wrong, and small quantities of the precious quicksilver, which ran gaily down the creek bed, were later retrieved by more "savvy" miners.

By this time, thousands of dollars had been poured into this still untested mine. When the mill began operating, it revealed the amount of gold was so trifling that only 10 of the 60 stamps were necessary. After only six days, the engines were shut down, never to resume. Everything but the gold output was perfect.

During these frantic activities, wives and investors arrived from France. They created quite a stir in the rough little mining town of Narbo, which was unused to cultured manners and a way of living as ridiculously extravagant as that of the mining operation.

Knowles. Traveling through Knowles, you are practically overwhelmed by the granite scattered over the countryside. Even fence posts were made from the rock, and a score of foundations serve as perpetual monuments for the wooden structures long since victims of decay, fire, and vandalism. Before the quarries stopped operating, much of the granite was used to rebuild San Francisco after the 1906 earthquake.

To reach Knowles, take back-country Road 415 from Coarsegold to Road 606 and jog south. To

return to Highway 49, follow Road 606 south a few miles to Road 600 and then turn northeast toward Raymond and Ahwahnee.

Raymond. The town was originally named Wildcat Station for an early-day tasty stew served to stage travelers on their way to Yosemite. Once terminus of a Southern Pacific spur line, today it is a quiet agricultural community with a minor quarry operation. The one-room jail still stands in the center of town.

For some varied scenery and some views of the past, follow the Ben Hur Road north of Raymond for 17 miles to Mormon Bar and State 49. A paved country road from Raymond leads 7 miles to the Ben Hur Road. As you gain in elevation, the road drops off steeply and views open up. About halfway along the route, you'll see paralleling the road a remarkably well-preserved stone fence, part of the 5-mile-long Clyde Quick Ranch fence, built in 1862 by Chinese laborers. Each was paid 25 cents a day to lay a required 25 feet of stone. Although the town of Ben Hur is still shown on many maps, it no longer exists as town or post office. As you continue north, you drive past small ranches, under shady oaks, and between rocks.

From Raymond, you can also return to Highway 49 just south of Ahwahnee via Road 600.

Grub Gulch. Another important gold discovery site of which little remains is Grub Gulch. Located 5 miles west of Ahwahnee on the road to Raymond (Road 600), today it is an open meadow with a few old rose bushes and an overgrown cemetery. Gaping holes in the hillside mark the sites of mines that lend credence to the claim that it was the largest mountain mining community in the southern section.

The Gambetta Mine, a decaying collection of crumbling buildings and rusted machinery northwest of the road, was the first and richest mine in town. It reportedly produced $490,000 in gold.

Hampered by lack of water, it was said whiskey was used to fight fires because of its greater availability. Although Grub Gulch never had a church, five saloons were active night and day.

Ahwahnee. Named for one of the Miwok Indian villages called *Awani*, Ahwahnee was a stage stop and later a farming community. Groves of apples, peaches, and pears dotted the valley around the turn of the century; today there are some traces of these orchards.

On a hillside less than a mile above the post office is an Indian burial ground, still in use.

Horses graze *on gently rolling hillside slopes along Ben Hur Road. Back-country fanciers will enjoy this alternate route (23 miles) between Raymond and Mariposa.*

Nearby, also on private property, stands the Roundhouse, a large wooden ceremonial meeting house. Still intact, it is the only one of its kind in existence in the West. Burned in 1893, as was customary at the death of an Indian chief, it was rebuilt in 1903.

Nipinnawasee. Most of the town of Nipinnawasee, 2 miles north of Ahwahnee, was burned in 1961. Perhaps the most distinctive feature of this cattle community is its Indian name which means "home of the deer."

MARIPOSA NORTH THROUGH COULTERVILLE

A new "gold rush" has begun in the area between Mariposa and Coulterville. Because of the proximity of this region to Yosemite National Park as well as several new water-oriented projects in conjunction with Lake McClure, traffic in the vicinity has increased. However, it is still one of the most isolated areas along State Highway 49.

There's still much to see of the original "Gold Rush." You'll find well-preserved buildings, mines,

tailings, and quartz formations, and Mariposa has an excellent museum. John C. Fremont had extensive holdings in the Mariposa and Bear Valley areas. Unfortunately, nothing remains of his house, but there are ruins of his "fort" and of a mine he claimed was his.

Most of the Gold Country towns are right on State 49; however, a side trip over to Hornitos — more Mexican in feeling than any other mining town in the Gold Country — and to La Grange — settled by French and heavily mined — will take you off the main route.

Driving this stretch of State 49 is slow because of the twisting highway. But you'll be rewarded with some spectacular scenic views, especially along the Merced River north of Bear Valley.

Mariposa. At the junction of State highways 49 and 140, Mariposa is far from a ghost town. It has a small, stable farming base, and the business district also gets a sizable amount of tourist traffic because of the town's convenient position halfway between Merced and Yosemite National Park.

An excellent historical center and museum on Jessie Street at the north end of town has displays depicting life as it was in Mariposa over a century ago. It is open daily (9 A.M. to 5 P.M.) from May

FREMONT—A WESTERN PIONEER

John C. Fremont was one of those who didn't make it in the California gold fields. Born in 1813, Fremont had a very busy early life. By the time gold was discovered in California, he had married the daughter of popular U. S. Senator Thomas Hart Benton, done some excellent topographic mapping of Missouri River territory, traveled the Rockies with Kit Carson, and led the first winter crossing of the Sierra.

In 1847, Fremont gave his agent, Thomas Larkin, $3,000 and instructions to buy an attractive piece of land near Mission San Jose where he could retire in peace from a tumultuous army career. But for some reason, Larkin instead bought 45,000 acres of dry land in the Sierra foothills for Fremont.

Fremont was livid, but soon found that gold had been discovered on his foothill land. When he realized the extent of the gold findings, the former soldier "floated" his original purchase up into the hills to take in even more gold-producing land, most of which had already been claimed by others. This gave him a single piece of property extending from the Merced River south to Bridgeport.

With this wealth behind him, Fremont moved into the political forefront and became one of California's leading citizens. He was the first (but unsuccessful) U. S. Presidential candidate of the fledgling Republican party in 1856.

In 1857, Fremont returned to his Mariposa land and found that absentee ownership, bad management, and costly lawsuits filed by miners who had been uprooted by Fremont's "floating" land grab were eating up all of the tremendous profits from the mining.

Fremont built a home at Bear Valley and settled down to enjoy the good life with his family and personally supervise his huge empire for a time. Although the mines produced at a record-breaking rate, there were no profits due to tremendous overhead costs, personal expenses, and legal involvements.

Fremont's very controversial military campaigning during the Civil War and his political opposition to Abraham Lincoln cost him his military commands, his political influence, and finally his public prestige. Unable to obtain new capital, finances at the Mariposa land went from bad to worse. Finally, in 1863, the property had to be sold for a fraction of its worth. Fremont received enough from the sale to live comfortably, but he managed to lose it all through unwise railroad speculations during the next decade. He died penniless in 1890 in New York, but he can scarcely be forgotten by future generations—his name has been given to more streets, towns, peaks, and landmarks than any other pioneer in Western history.

through September and most weekends during the rest of the year. The community has managed to preserve several Gold Rush buildings. Right on the main street are the Trabucco warehouse and store, the I.O.O.F. Hall, and the balconied Schlageter Hotel, which has been converted into stores and offices.

One block east of the main street is the old stone jail, once the largest in the entire Mother Lode. The 30 by 50-foot granite block structure has not been out of service for too many years, and it looks just as sturdy as ever.

The choicest architectural building in Mariposa is above the commercial section on a quiet hill at the north end of town. The two-story wooden courthouse, oldest in continuous operation in the state (since 1854), has been recognized as one of the Mother Lode's finest buildings since the day it opened. Remodeled only slightly, the building's classically simple lines and stark white walls never fail to impress visitors. The courtroom still has many of its original furnishings. The original clock in the tower has tolled out the hours since 1866.

Mariposa ("butterfly" in Spanish) was once

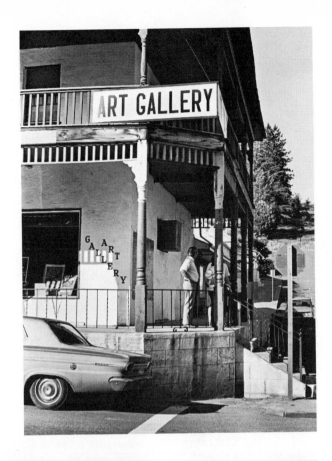

Mariposa offers *tourists a range of attractions — from good examples of Gold Rush architecture (the balconied Schlageter Hotel,* **top left,** *and St. Joseph's Catholic church,* **bottom right**) *to a museum* **(bottom left)** *with a replica of famed Mary Harrison Mine, and an amphitheater* **(top right)** *where summer repertory companies perform.*

In sleepy Hornitos, *the small white Catholic church, buttressed in stone, still stands as a guardian of the little cemetery. Among the tombstones, you'll find reminders of the more rowdy Gold Rush days.*

Traveler peers *into windows of deserted Chowchilla School on State 49 between Nipinnawasee and Usona.*

part of the 45,000 acre tract belonging to John C. Fremont (see page 22). It has served as seat of Mariposa County since 1851.

The Mariposa Mine, near the south end of town, discovered by Kit Carson and Alex Gody in 1849, supplied the first steam quartz mill in California. (You can see the entrance to the mine from the back of St. Joseph's Catholic Church.) Gold production continued into the twentieth century and actually hit its peak between 1900 and 1915.

Other prosperous mining camps around Mariposa included Mormon Bar, Bootjack, and Agua Fria—now just picturesque names.

Mount Bullion. As with so many town sites along the Gold Country roads, there is little left at Mount Bullion to suggest the fevered activity of the 2,000 men who first worked the placers in 1850 and then turned to the rich quartz veins in their search for gold. Trabucco's store is still open; the Princeton Saloon and Mount Bullion School buildings are only reminders of busier days.

The now-vanished Princeton Mine, which produced more than $4 million, was located just south of the present town site.

Mount Ophir. The site of Mount Ophir is marked by a few crumbling stone ruins along a stretch of the old highway that parallels the present route of State 49 north of Mount Bullion.

It was at Mount Ophir in 1850 that John L. Moffatt, blessed with official authorization of the United States government, operated the first private mint in California. The mint supposedly produced $50 hexagonal gold slugs (none of which have been found), a more convenient means of exchange than the traditional gold dust.

Hornitos. A side trip west of State 49 takes you to Hornitos, a once roaring, lawless town and a particularly rewarding stop. Not only are there several old buildings still standing around the Mexican-style plaza, but the town is rich in history and colorful anecdotes. Hornitos was considered one of the rowdiest towns ever spawned during the Gold Rush, and it supposedly was the favorite haunt of Joaquin Murieta, certainly the most storied outlaw of early California (see page 27).

Founded by Mexican miners who had been "voted" out of neighboring Quartzburg by a law-and-order committee of Americans, Hornitos reflects Mexican influence more than any other Gold Country settlement. The town's name means "little ovens" in Spanish and presumably was named after the little oven-shaped tombs that the first settlers built above the ground for the dead. Some of these unusual graves can still be seen in a special little graveyard that has been fenced off below St. Catherine's Church (built in 1862).

You can still view Hornitos' first jail, a small building with 2-foot-thick granite walls, and the closed fronts of numerous general stores, warehouses, and anonymous buildings that may once have been saloons, fandango halls, or gambling places. Some still carry bullet holes from former gun battles.

In the center of town, across from the plaza, are the remains of one of the first stores operated by D. Ghirardelli & Co., the well-known San Francisco chocolate makers. Only the walls of the old store, built in 1859, still stand.

According to a local report, one of the adobes on the west side of the main street at the north end of town was an opium den of considerable disrepute.

Local legend places Murieta as a frequent visitor to the wild old town. He was supposed to have had his own secret tunnel as an escape route from the fandango hall when circumstances got too hot above the ground. The entrance is now clearly marked at the corner of High Street and Bear Valley Road. In contradiction to this colorful story, the practical contention is that this tunnel was used to roll beer barrels from a cellar storeroom to the basement of the dance hall.

In Spanish, *Hornitos means "little ovens," probably referring to the unusual-shaped tombs on boot hill.*

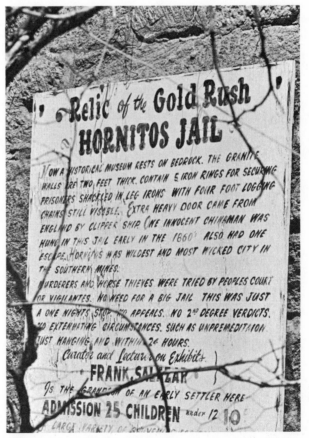

History *of Hornitos' small jail (open occasionally) is told by plaque on its 2-foot-thick stone walls.*

Hornitos' reputation for wildness has been enhanced by stories like that of the two gamblers (one version says they were women fandango dancers) who wrapped shirts (or shawls) around their arms as shields and duelled with gleaming knives in a vacant lot until they killed each other before a cheering audience of miners.

But the tragic tale of the Chinese, who in a moment of rage fired a pistol to frighten a tormenting white boy and by accident slightly wounded him, is one which few stories still told in the Gold Country can match. The Chinese figured that his chances would be best if he headed for the hills, but he was soon caught by a posse and escorted to the Hornitos jail. Angry miners realized that it would be difficult, if not impossible, to break into the vault-like building, so with grisly ingenuity they lured the pitiful prisoner to the cell's tiny window with the promise of tobacco, then seized him, threw a noose around his neck, and by violently jerking the rope literally dashed his brains out against the stone wall.

Incidentally, Quartzburg failed to survive despite its self-righteousness (or perhaps because of it). The now-abandoned town site is about 3 miles northeast of Hornitos on the Bear Valley Road.

Bear Valley. The few buildings left in Bear Valley don't speak of the days when John Charles Fremont (see page 22) "owned" the town and ruled his sizable empire from the residence he staffed with French servants for his wife and children. Nor do they tell of the 3,000 souls who lived in the little city when local quartz was yielding gold in abundance.

The ruins that still sit beside the highway (State 49) include the Bon Ton Saloon (now a restaurant), a boarding house, the Garbarino store, the I.O.O.F. Hall which houses the Oso Museum, and Trabucco's store. Unfortunately, there are no signs of Fremont's home or of the famed Oso House, a balconied hostelry built in 1850 of lumber brought around the Horn, where Fremont's friends stayed. Only rock fragments remain of the Chinese settlement north of town.

Historical photos *depict life in Bear Valley and Coulterville around the time of John C. Fremont.* **Above** *is his home, the "White House," and* **at bottom right** *he sits atop a stage in front of Oso House, a hotel built to house his visitors. The steam engine being hauled by mule team ran between Coulterville and the Mary Harrison Mine, 4 miles north of town.*

THE LEGENDARY JOAQUIN MURIETA

Fanciful "portrait" ignores reality.

Joaquin Murieta was the most romantic figure of the California Gold Rush. Immortalized in books, paintings, innumerable anecdotes, and even a Hollywood motion picture, Murieta emerged as Robin Hood of the Southern Mines, avenger of his murdered family, friend of the poor, and defender of his countrymen.

The legend of Joaquin Murieta is still very much alive. Visitors to the Gold Country will find his name inscribed on historical markers and plaques, and his heroic feats recounted endlessly by yarn spinners. Saw Mill Flat, outside of Sonora, claims to be the place where Murieta first settled when he arrived from Sonora, Mexico, in 1850. It was in Murphys that the handsome young man allegedly swore vengeance against his Yankee persecutors after they tied him to a tree and beat him bloody, then ravished his wife and murdered his brother.

Residents of San Andreas tell how a Frenchman made Murieta's famous bulletproof vest, and then had to prove its effectiveness by wearing it while Joaquin shot at him from point blank range. In Hornitos, there is an underground tunnel supposedly used by the bandit to escape hotly-pursuing lawmen. Outside of Volcano, there used to be a well-disguised treehouse where Joaquin is said to have hidden while puzzled rangers milled around beneath him. Mokelumne Hill and Sonora also claim to be the scenes of Murieta's wild escapades.

According to the legend, Murieta died in a blaze of glory in 1853. He was hunted down by a lawman named Harry Love and shot to death in southern Mariposa County. Love cut off the bandit's head, put it in a bottle of alcohol, and used it as proof to claim a reward.

How much of this legend is true? Tellers of tales swear that it's all true. Local residents admit that maybe a few of the details have been fabricated. Some historians accept only part of the legend. Other historians, notably Joseph Henry Jackson, claim that it's all a fairy tale. In his book, *Bad Company,* and in other writings, Jackson has carefully traced the origins of the Murieta legend to the flowery pens of imaginative authors.

There are a few facts involved, but not many. In 1852 and 1853, the Southern Mines were bothered by a number of thieves, all named Joaquin. Authorities arriving at the scene of a crime would ask, "Who did it?" Most often, the answer was simply "Joaquin."

In response to public outcries, the state legislature really did hire Harry Love in May, 1853, to get a bandit named Joaquin—no last name specified—and offered $5,000 as reward. Love took the job but didn't have much luck for several weeks. Finally he surprised a group of Mexicans around their campfire one night and killed a few, including an unnamed man who claimed to be their leader. Love decapitated the man, named him Joaquin Murieta out of desperation, and went back to claim his reward.

The legislature paid off, but not everyone was convinced of the head's identity. A surviving member of the Mexican gang claimed that it belonged to Joaquin Valenzuela. Some of Murieta's supposed "relatives" were brought forth by authorities to identify the deceased. But others who knew Joaquin Murieta claimed that the grisly prize bore no resemblance to the man.

It was about a year after this confusion died down that the legend of Joaquin Murieta was born, according to Jackson. A writer named John Rollin Ridge dreamed up a book called *The Life and Adventures of Joaquin Murieta, the Celebrated California Bandit.* Ridge made up the whole wild story, including many of the details now accepted as fact, and then cleverly ended the sordid tale by having the criminal killed and decapitated by Harry Love.

During the next century, the Murieta legend was revived many times, with each new writer basing his research not on fact, but on Ridge's tale. With each retelling, a few details were added. Over the years, Joaquin grew handsomer, was able to trace his lineage to Montezuma, and displayed some new tricks that he had learned from a friend named Kit Carson.

The Gold Rush needs a romantic hero, and the mythical Murieta fills the need. History notwithstanding, it seems certain that the legendary Joaquin Murieta will not die—or even suffer a serious illness—for a long time to come.

Hollow shells *of Bear Valley buildings reflect the effects of years of neglect and exposure to elements.*

Traces *of Pine Tree Mine, remnants of John C. Fremont's "empire," are visible from Hell's Hollow grade.*

About 2 miles south of Bear Valley, you can catch a glimpse of the Mother Lode quartz formations through the trees west of State 49. Two miles north of the town is a highway pull-out that affords excellent views of the Merced River gorge below. From here the sinuous road begins a thousand-foot descent into what was called Hell's Hollow. About halfway down the grade are the remains of the Pine Tree Mine, one of John Fremont's most disputed holdings. Historians exploring the scrub-covered hillsides west of this mine found what is believed to be the crumbling foundations of Fremont's "fort," built in the 1850's to help defend his mining empire against encroachment. Just north of here was Bagby, once the site of California's first power dam and Fremont's stamp mill; it now lies under the waters of Lake McClure and is designated the Bagby Recreation Area.

Coulterville. Rival store-owners George W. Coulter and George Maxwell arrived at this Mexican mining community around the same time. In 1849, Coulter pitched a tent at this site from which flew an American flag. The Mexicans called it "Banderita" (little flag), the first name of the camp. Ignoring this name, Coulter and Maxwell drew lots to see which pioneer would be commemorated; Maxwell lost but had his name affixed to the near-by creek and the first post office. Coulter's frame home still stands northeast of town.

The Jeffery Hotel, the town's most imposing structure, is neither stately nor preposterous in appearance, but just about halfway between. The building was converted into a hotel by George Jeffery in 1870 from a Mexican structure of rock and adobe built in 1851. The old walls are 3 feet thick. The Magnolia Saloon next door contains a fine collection of firearms, minerals, coins, and other Gold Rush items.

Across the street are the remains of the Coulter Hotel and the Wells Fargo building that served as a trading post during the boom days when there were 25 saloons on the main street. Nelson Cody, the brother of Buffalo Bill, operated the business in the Wells Fargo building during the 1870's and also served as postmaster for a long time.

In front of these buildings are the local "hangin' tree" and a small steam engine that was used at the Mary Harrison Mine north of town to haul ore along a 4-mile stretch of track known as the world's crookedest railroad. You can still see part of the boiler house and foundation of this famous old mine that was opened in the 1860's and produced until 1903; drive south out of Coulterville on State 49 and turn right on the first black-topped road

"Whistling Billy" once hauled ore but now rests in Coulterville square. Jeffery Hotel is in background.

(about a mile from town). The mine shaft was once 1,200 feet deep, with 15 levels and 15 miles of drifts (side tunnels).

At one time, there was a sizable Chinese population in Coulterville. One Chinese adobe, the Sun Sun Wo store, can still be found among the scattered residences east of town.

Coulterville has been gutted by three fires. The last blaze indirectly caused the village's last and perhaps the country's shortest "Gold Rush." In 1899, rubble of a stone-and-adobe building that was razed after the conflagration was used to fill chuckholes in the street. Apparently unknown to anyone living here was a secret cache of gold coins in the very walls being used for fill. With the first rain, several of these coins were exposed by the running water and the rush was on. As the story goes, the town's populace turned out armed with shovels, picks, butcher knives, spoons, and other improbable mining tools, and quickly reduced the street to a state of impassable confusion.

La Grange. The village of La Grange, located west of Coulterville on the banks of the Tuolumne River, is flanked by immense tailing piles that testify to the heavy mining activity that characterized the area for more than half a century.

The town was settled in 1852 by a group of French miners and was logically named French Bar. When the gold gave out on the bar, the center of activity was moved up the hill, and commerce replaced the pick and shovel. There was a population of about 5,000 at the town's business peak, and La Grange even served as seat of Stanislaus County from 1855 to 1862. Three major stage lines made regular stops here.

There are only a few Gold Rush buildings left in town. Near the east end of the present business district is a large stone building and the remains of the old adobe post office (now incorporated into a barn). At the opposite end of town is the wooden I.O.O.F. Hall.

BIG OAK FLAT AREA NORTH THROUGH JAMESTOWN

Most Gold Rush reminders in the area lie in intriguing side trips short distances off State 49. To the east on State Highway 120, you'll climb up Big Oak Flat and visit towns that now belong to history. To the west, on the Stanislaus River, is one of California's remaining covered bridges, at Knights Ferry. Excluding side excursions, the actual distance on State 49 between Moccasin and Jamestown is less than 15 miles.

Browsing through the town sites, you'll find some preserved buildings, crumbling ruins of others. In Chinese Camp, you'll see the Oriental influence in the locust-like trees. An interesting cemetery marks Stent. Jamestown offers blockhouses, a grist mill, a mine, and the restored Sierra Railway depot and yards.

Two famous visitors to the area were Bret Harte, who supposedly used Second Garrote as the locale for a story, and U. S. Grant, whose in-laws had a house at Knights Ferry.

Priest. At the Moccasin Creek Power Plant, State Highway 120 intersects with State 49. Turning east onto State 120, you climb steadily for 12 miles along a historic section of the Mother Lode. From State 120, the old, winding Priest Grade Road, still open to traffic, is easily viewed. At the top of the first steep grade was the town of Priest, a one-time supply base for miners in the area and site of a famous hotel, which was a stopping place for travelers to Yosemite. Now destroyed by fire, only a motel and cafe mark the town site.

Big Oak Flat. The gold-laden gravels that made Big Oak Flat a rich placer camp were discovered

SAVAGE—SOLDIER, MINER, TRADER

Soldier, miner, Indian trader, leader of the famed Mariposa Battalion, and first explorer of Yosemite Valley, James Savage spent considerable time in the southern part of the Gold Country. However, his first destination in California was Sutter's Fort, where he arrived in 1846 with an emigrant party from Illinois. The hardships of that trip claimed the lives of his wife and child.

After a few months as a soldier in John C. Fremont's California Battalion, he went to work for John Sutter at his fort, and Sutter's diary records that Savage worked with Marshall on the construction of the now-famous mill.

In 1848, he drifted southward and began mining and trading with the Indians at Woods Diggings and Jamestown. Discovering that a fortune could be made by supplying goods in exchange for gold, Savage made friends with the Indians and learned many of their dialects.

In the spring of 1850, Savage was warned that the Indians had decided to drive the invaders from their land. Raids were made on his trading posts on Mariposa Creek and on the Fresno River, 4 miles from the present site of Coarsegold. Several of his employees were murdered. Although it was first thought this was Savage's private war, 74 volunteer miner-fighters responded to a call for help.

When the Mariposa Battalion was formed, James Savage was made a major. On patrol on March 25, 1851, Savage and his men entered Yosemite Valley and became its first white explorers. They captured Chief Tenaya.

Major Savage resumed his trading and regained the allegiance of the Indians through a combination of awe and fear. He used little magic tricks like burning oil on a pan of water and claiming he had the power to burn up all the rivers. He was also reputed to use a battery to give the Indians a shock, whereby he declared he had the powers of great gods. His popularity and prosperity aroused much jealousy and Major Walter H. Harvey, a rival trader, spearheaded an attack where several Indians were killed. Savage asserted Harvey was responsible for their deaths and took Harvey up on a boast that Savage was afraid to visit on Harvey's own territory. During a fist fight, Savage's pistol fell from his shirt and during the scuffle Harvey killed Savage.

Some questions remain unanswered, among them what happened to the fortune Savage supposedly acquired in his prosperous trading posts. When his grave was opened all that was found, in addition to fragments of bones, was a piece of Chinese pottery, a rusted squirrel trap, broken bits of glass bottles, and a piece of metal framework for an old-fashioned purse.

late in 1849 by James Savage (see box at left), whose company included five Indian wives and several Indian servants. This is the same Savage who explored Yosemite Valley a year later while leading a group of volunteers in pursuit of less friendly Indians.

The abundance of stone and adobe ruins found today in Big Oak Flat is far out of proportion to the present size of the village, and it is not difficult to imagine the extent of the boom town that developed after Savage's discovery.

A large oak tree was the distinguishing feature of the area. In the frenzied search for gold, miners reduced the gravels of the flat some 5 feet, removing the earth around the tree which eventually toppled over. A few sections of wood from this tree are preserved in a stone monument along State 120 at the west end of town.

Groveland. Originally called Garrote in honor of the hanging of a horse thief that took place in 1850, the name Groveland first appeared in the 1870's and presumably was chosen by a calmer populace.

The building now known as the Iron Door and a former grocery store date back to the 1850's. An historic old hotel has been refurbished and is used as headquarters for land developers in the area.

Second Garrote. Supposedly some 60 men were hanged from a tree, giving this small mining community its name, but the tree is gone, and there is no historical basis for this claim.

An old cabin in the area was known as "Bret Harte's Cabin" and was supposedly the setting for his story "Tennessee's Partner." Two young settlers here, Jason P. Chamberlain and John A. Chaffee, were supposedly the models for the protagonists in the short story. Although the cabin burned several years ago, the legend refuses to die. Chamberlain and Chaffee were young men when they settled in Second Garrote in 1852. Here they built a two-story frame house and lived as inseparable friends for the next 51 years. Long before Chaffee died in 1903, their reputation for loyalty to each other and kindness to travelers that passed on Big Oak Flat Road became a legend. Chamberlain lived on for three months after Chaffee's death, but finally took his own life, heartbroken and lonely.

Jacksonville. A parking area and a marker near the new State 120 bridge tell the tale of Jacksonville, a once-important gold town now inundated by the Don Pedro Reservoir. Named for Colonel A. M. Jackson who opened a trading post in 1849, it was the site of the large Shawmut Mine and the second largest town in Tuolumne County in 1850. Here thousands of miners once feverishly worked the rich beds of the Tuolumne River.

Chinese Camp. One of the most famous and most popular of the southern Gold Rush towns is Chinese Camp, which sits like an oasis amid grass and tarweed fields on State 49. There are some good ruins to explore, and one of the wildest fights ever staged in the foothills took place about 3 miles west of town.

No one really knows just where the Chinese who settled here came from. They may have been employed by English prospectors, or they could have been part of one of the many ship's crews that deserted in San Francisco during the early days of the Gold Rush. At any rate, there were no less than 5,000 Chinese mining the area in the early 1850's.

Trouble came to Chinese Camp in 1856. According to local history, it all started when a huge stone rolled from the diggings of one group to an area where another group was working. A fight developed, and when it ended, the squabbling groups sent out a call for help to their respective tongs — the Sam Yap and the Yan Wo. Each faction felt it had lost face and the only proper thing to do was stage a full scale war between the two tongs.

Preparations were hurriedly made, and each side built up an arsenal of crude weapons. Local blacksmiths fashioned spears, tridents, battle axes, pikes, and daggers. A few muskets were brought from San Francisco, and Yankee miners were hired to instruct the combatants in the use of these strange instruments of destruction.

Finally, all was ready. On October 25, 1856, 1,200 members of the Sam Yap fraternity met 900

Old-time post office *along Chinese Camp's main street is still in use (note zip code). Locust-like trees in background are Chinese trees of heaven, planted in profusion wherever the Chinese settled.*

Covered bridge *at Knights Ferry is one of few left in the state. Ruins of a grist mill are just beyond.*

Chinese Camp *looks its age; the Catholic church and graveyard have seen more than a century of service.*

Yan Wo brothers. Bolstered by speeches and some fire water, the two groups lined up and went for each other, hammer and tong.

When the smoke cleared, four persons were dead — most likely trampled to death — and another dozen were injured. About 250 were taken prisoner by local American law authorities. The war was over, stature was regained, and everybody went back to the mines.

Perhaps the most noticeable feature of Chinese Camp today is a profusion of locust-like trees. These are Chinese trees of heaven, planted wherever Chinese settled in the Gold Country. In the shade of the delicate branches, you'll find the post office (still in use), the Wells Fargo Express building (in ruins), and an old store. The graveyard is near picturesque St. Francis Xavier Catholic Church on the east side of the highway.

A little side trip northwest from Chinese Camp on State Highway 108 follows the old Sonora Road. It is said that campfires were so numerous along this trail in 1849 that travelers needed no other light to mark their route except the embers of those who had gone ahead.

Remains of an old irrigation system at Yosemite Junction, 4 miles west of Chinese Camp on State Highway 108, mark the site of a once-flourishing agricultural area. Vegetables from here were sent over Sonora Pass to Bodie during that mining camp's heyday. Watch for stone corrals alongside the road — all that remain of Keystone and Cri-

mea house, two old-time stage stations, still shown on some maps.

Knights Ferry. Scout and fur trader William Knight started the first ferry operation across the Stanislaus River in 1848 to take advantage of the Gold Rush traffic. Thousands of miners passed this way, and ferry receipts easily totaled $500 a day. Knights Ferry was located in the center of a rich area with gold being discovered along river bars and banks, hills and gulches, for several miles in each direction.

John and Lewis Dent took over the operation in 1849 after Knight was killed in a gunfight, and later they built a grist mill and sawmill downstream from the long covered bridge that now crosses the river just above town. When the town was formally established in 1856, there was some effort to call it Dentville, but Knights Ferry was well-established.

The town's greatest fame derives from a visit by U. S. Grant in 1854. Grant was married to Julia Dent, and he lived with his in-laws during his short stay. The original Dent House still stands in the shade of tall locusts about a block from the main section of town.

The covered bridge you see today was not the first one across the river. The original, built in 1854, was washed away in the floods of 1862, and the present bridge went up soon after in the same place — but eight feet higher. The grist mill that now stands in ruins also is a replacement for the original that was swept down the river along with the bridge.

Two of the most conspicuous Gold Rush buildings that are still standing are the iron jailhouse and the Masonic Hall.

Stent. This rather recent name was given to the historic village of Utterville. Although the area was known as Poverty Hill, it was once a busy camp serving the Jumper, Golden Rule, and other profitable mines. When the gold gave out, so did the settlement. It managed to hang on until the turn of the century, but a fire in 1906 destroyed more than a hundred houses and sealed the town's fate. Today, the only Gold Rush reminder is a neglected old cemetery by the schoolhouse.

Stent sits to the east of the Jacksonville Road.

Quartz. All of Quartz's old buildings burned in a 1927 fire, and now there are only a few residential buildings to mark the site of the very productive App Mine. John App, who started the mining in 1856, achieved a measure of fame when he married Leanna Donner, one of the six Donner girls orphaned by the Donner Pass tragedy in 1847.

Mrs. App lived in the original homestead until her death in 1930. The house can still be seen east of State 49 on the narrow road between Quartz and Jamestown.

Jamestown. The first gold discovery in Tuolumne County was made in August of 1848 on Woods Creek, 1 mile south of Jamestown. For a time, miners were taking out $200 to $300 a day with a pick and knife. It is said more gold was taken from this creek than any other stream its size in California. A marker in town commemorates the discovery of a 75-pound nugget.

The settlement was founded in 1848 by Colonel George James, a lawyer from San Francisco. James was not known for his scruples, and he was finally forced to leave by disgruntled citizens who objected to all the high-handedness. The town even tried to change its name to American Camp, but "Jimtown" was too firmly fixed to be legislated out of existence.

"Jimtown" seems to be trying valiantly to retain its antiquity. Some of its best wood-frame buildings were destroyed in a tragic fire in November, 1966, but there are still a few wood structures from the 1870's and 1880's, plus some fire-resistant blockhouses dating from the 1850's. The fancy gingerbread and brick Emporium on Main Street and the Community Methodist Church with its quaint belfry, one-half block west of Main Street, are among the most photogenic. The res-

toration of the Sierra Railway depot and yards was completed in 1971. This line, which formerly connected the Mother Lode mines with shipping centers in the San Joaquin Valley, is now known as Rail Town 1897. Tours of the 5-acre park of railroad memorabilia on 5th Avenue are conducted daily between 10 A.M. and 4 P.M. during the summer, weekends during spring and fall. There is a small admission fee. (See pages 34-35.)

There is a good view of Table Mountain, an ancient lava mass roughly a quarter mile wide and 40 miles long, on the Rawhide Road. Mining tunnels honeycomb most of the mountain. The Humbug Mine, on the mountain's eastern slope, yielded some $4 million and nuggets the size of hen's eggs.

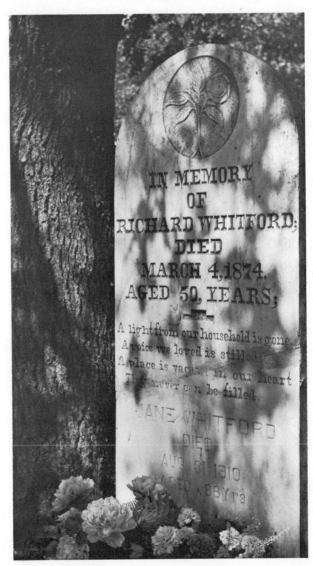

Old cemetery *in Stent is the only link with the past when miners dug fortunes from the surrounding hills.*

Steam whistles can still be heard in the Gold Country. Echoing through the hills, they now signal the beginning or end of a ride on one of four old railroad lines whose main activity is carrying visitors. In the late 1800's, their freight was primarily timber and supplies, hauled to and from old logging camps.

On these short journeys backwards into history, you'll see restored rolling stock, picturesque stations, and scenery along the route. Take along a picnic lunch—there's always a place to eat.

Following are the four railroad lines and their depot locations.

Jamestown. The Sierra Railroad, built in 1897 to connect the mines of the Mother Lode with freight centers in the San Joaquin Valley, is still an operating standard-gauge railroad. The classic depot, offices, roundhouse, shops, yards, and trains are now open to the public as Rail Town 1897. Step through the door of the depot and you're in another century—furniture, tickets, everything needed to "run a railroad" looks as it did in 1897.

In addition to looking around the depot and museum upstairs, there is a guided tour of the roundhouse and shops where you can see the machinery run and learn how the track was made. The star attractions are the locomotives. No. 3, one of the line's original iron horses, is a 4-6-0 Rogers, built in 1891. It's the Hooterville Cannonball of *Petticoat Junction* fame. No. 28, a 2-8-0 Baldwin, built in 1922, is used for excursion runs.

Admission, which includes everything but a train ride, is $1 for adults, 50 cents for children 8 to 18, children under 8, free; maximum family admission, $2.50. Rail Town is open every day but Monday during the summer from 10 A.M. to 4 P.M. and weekends from April to June and Labor Day through the first weekend in November.

Twelve-mile round-trip train rides begin the end of April. Trains leave from 11 A.M. to 3 P.M. Tickets are $2.50 for adults, $1.25 for children, under 8 are free; maximum family fare is $6.25.

For information on schedules and Saturday night dinner excursions write Great Western Tours, 495 Geary Street, San Francisco 94109.

Tuolumne. The West Side & Cherry Valley Railway chugs out of Tuolumne (about 10 miles east of Sonora) on tracks constructed in 1896 by Chinese laborers. Once used to bring lumber from the mountains to a mill at Tuolumne, a portion of the narrow-gauge lines were retained for the pleasure of people who treasure the memory of steam railroading. Two Shay locomotives were restored, 1899 logging flat cars were turned into touring coaches, and the original railroad car and engine shops were again put to use.

The line operates two trips daily, at 10 A.M. and 12:30 P.M., Thursday through Monday, from the middle of June until the middle of September. The 12-mile round-trip takes about 2 hours. Tickets are $3.50 for adults, $2 for children 5 through 15; children under 5, free.

Steam engine pulls into Jamestown depot.

Engineer explains "railroad time."

From Memorial Day until the middle of June and from the middle of September through October, there is one trip (12:30 P.M.) on weekends only. Also on weekends throughout the season, you can make a longer trip (18¼ miles) to Toyon Park on the North Fork of the Tuolumne. There's a 2½ hour layover for picnicking or swimming, or for trying a little gold panning. Tickets are $7 for adults and $5 for children.

In Tuolumne, youngsters can try their skill at blowing the large mill whistle powered by an old Willamette steam donkey engine. There is a logging museum with free movies, a blacksmith shop, gift shop, and steam engine display.

For reservations and additional information, write to West Side & Cherry Valley Railway, P. O. Box 1017, Tuolumne, California 95379.

Lyons Lake Resort. Sixteen miles east of Sonora off State Highway 108, Lyons Lake Resort offers speeder train rides on an old logging railroad. It's only 4 miles round trip, but plan on spending over an hour as many stops are made along the way.

From the first of May through September, the trains operate seven days a week, with trips scheduled at 11 A.M., 2 P.M., and 5 P.M. Tickets are $2 for adults, $1 for children 5 to 16; children under 5, free. When the track is extended to Middle Fence Road, prices will probably be increased.

At Lyons Lake, there's boating, camping and picnicking sites, and a children's playground. For a brochure, write to Lyons Lake Resort, Star Route, P. O. Box 1196, Sonora, California 95370.

Camino. The Camino, Cable & Northern Railroad is located in the little mountain town of Camino, 6 miles east of Placerville, on U. S. Highway 50. Once its slim-gauge lines were part of the vast network of the narrow-gauge which laced the high country of the West.

Its forerunner was built near the turn of the century by the El Dorado Lumber Company to connect a sawmill at Pino Grande with the planing mill at Camino. Until the original tracks were removed in 1951, the woods and orchards from Camino to Cable heard the sound of bells, whistles, and hissing steam as the diminutive locomotives hauled heavy loads of cut timber to the storage yard and railhead at Camino.

Today, the Camino, Cable & Northern Railroad follows that same right of way. It's only a few miles round trip now but will eventually be extended to the old lumber camp of Cable, more than 1,200 feet above the American River.

The train operates weekends from 11:15 A.M. to 4:15 P.M., May through October (or "until the snow flies"). Your ticket allows stopover privileges at the Apple Hill Picnic Grounds so you can get off, eat, and visit the railroad museum with its large display of narrow-gauge equipment. Trains come by every hour.

Fares are $1.25 for adults, $1 for students 13 to 18, and 75 cents for children through 12. For a complete schedule, write CC&N Railroad, Camino, California 95709.

Interior has many view seats.

All aboard for a short run at Camino.

LOOP TRIP FROM SONORA

Bustling Sonora offers a great deal of history behind her modern façade and provides a variety of accommodations for travelers. It is a good base camp for exploring much of the colorful surrounding countryside.

Your loop trip takes you through Columbia State Park, a careful restoration of one of the Gold Country's wildest communities. Activities today match those that took place over a century ago — panning for gold, riding a stagecoach, having a sarsaparilla at a saloon.

Beautiful frame *building at the north end of Sonora is St. James Episcopal Church, over 100 years old.*

James Fair, who went on to fame and fortune with the Comstock Lode in Nevada, got his start at Shaws Flat. In Tuttletown, you can view the ruins of a store where Mark Twain came to shop and where Bret Harte was a clerk. Over in Jackass Hill, Mark Twain lived for five months in a cabin and wrote about the jumping frog.

Sonora. In the early 1850's, Sonora and Columbia battled it out for preeminence. Today, there is no question about which is the liveliest — Sonora is booming still and has one of the busiest main streets to be found in the Mother Lode. As the seat of Tuolumne County and a trading center for the surrounding cattle and lumber country, Sonora is as bustling as it was more than a century ago.

Sonora's early history was marred by some ugly incidents between the Mexicans and the Yankees. The town originally was settled early in 1848 by Mexicans and was known as Sonorian Camp. More Mexicans settled quickly but the Americans weren't far behind, and they did their best to drive off the "furriners" from the south. The vindictive state-wide $20-a-month tax on foreigners was aimed principally at Mexican miners, causing them to band together in defiance. Although there was scattered violence, the Mexicans realized they were beaten and left town in a mass exodus.

Sonora's population dropped from 5,000 to 3,000 practically overnight, and the business community suffered hard times until the tax was repealed in 1851 and Mexicans once again felt safe to return to town.

During its peak production period, Sonora became the Queen of the Southern Mines and one of the wildest towns in the foothills. Washington Street was lined haphazardly with buildings made of adobe, hewn planks, sailcloth, and tin. Horse races and bull-and-bear fights were common, and there was no lack of painted ladies. Liquid refreshment was readily available at any hour of the day or night.

Today, modern façades cover the aged buildings, and traffic moves slowly along crowded Washington Street. But even with its modern face, much of Sonora reflects the old days. Just drive a block off the main street and you'll find yourself stepping backward a century. Stewart Street, east of and parallel to Washington, is one of the best routes for this type of leisurely exploration.

Unquestionably, the outstanding piece of old architecture in Sonora is St. James Episcopal Church, which stands at the head of Washington Street on the north end of town. It's not the oldest building in town, but it's the most elegant.

WHITE-WATER BOATING—LIGHT BOATS ON FAST WATER

The rivers of the Gold Rush Country are among the favorite waterways of an active group of kayakers, canoers, and raft riders who enjoy "white-water boating."

The thrill of white-water boating comes from maneuvering a light craft down a river that has enough current, waves, twists, and turns to pose a real challenge to the boater. It can be enjoyed on any river that is deep enough for the boats, but is not too steep or rocky. Several rivers in the California foothills fit these requirements.

Each river is classified according to its difficulty, on an international scale of I (the easiest) to VI (only for experts). In some cases, two sections of the same river may fall into different classifications because of changes in grade or water conditions.

Here are the classifications assigned to some popular Gold Rush Country rivers:

North Fork of the Feather River near Belden, Class IV to V, is the site of the National Slalom and Downriver races. The slalom is primarily a test of boating skill on a marked course. Contestants must navigate some gates while traveling downstream, others while moving upstream, and still others backward. The course is about ¼-mile long; 18 gates is the minimum. The downriver race is on a grueling, 6-mile course with seven big rapids. However, the Feather River between Oroville and its junction with the Sacramento River is Class II at the upper end, Class I farther downstream, and suitable for beginners and intermediates.

Sacramento River between Redding and Red Bluff is Class I-II. This is a popular two-day run for kayaks, canoes, and rafts.

The lower Yuba River from State Highway 20 bridge to Daguerra Dam at Browns Valley is Class I or II—a very nice one-day trip.

Bear River is small, but there is enough water in the spring for some good boating; this is Class I-II. Boats can be put in the water near the State Highway 65 bridge near Wheatland and taken out at a county road downstream.

South Fork of the American River is very popular with kayak groups. The Coloma-Lotus area is Class II and III; upstream from Coloma and downstream from Lotus, the river is Class III-IV.

Cosumnes River is small but good for spring and early summer boating, particularly in the Bridgehouse-Sloughhouse area. Upstream from Bridgehouse, the river is too steep and rocky.

American River near Fair Oaks is Class I and II—an excellent place for beginners. There are several good access points.

Mokelumne River has one very nice boating section (Class II or III) above State Highway 49. Boats can be put in at the Electra Powerhouse and taken out at the highway bridge.

Stanislaus River is Class II and III from Parrots Ferry to State 49. The river is in a beautiful and isolated canyon above Parrots Ferry, but the rough water is suitable only for experts and commercial rafters.

Beginners will do well to join one of the organized groups that take frequent trips on the Gold Country rivers. The largest organization is the River Touring Section of the Mother Lode Chapter of the Sierra Club (P. O. Box 1335, Sacramento, California 95806). In addition to arranging several trips a year, this group conducts classes in paddling techniques, safety, water reading, equipment, and self-rescue.

Inner tube riders try Mokelumne River below Electra Powerhouse.

Sonora's Chinatown *is gone, except for one old building off Main Street that was once a dry goods store. Note the typical Gold Rush architecture: brick front, stone sides, and heavy iron door.*

Notice the beautifully-restored house across from the church.

Other notable buildings in town include the I.O.O.F. Hall and the City Hotel. Several old structures were destroyed by fire in 1969. On Washington Street at the south end of town stands the Gunn House, the oldest residence in Sonora. Built by Dr. Lewis C. Gunn in 1850 for his family, it later became the offices for the *Sonora Herald*, the first newspaper in the mining area. Now remodeled, it is operated as an inn (see pages 58-59). The Tuolumne County Historical Society Museum is housed in the century-old jail on West Bradford Street.

The Big Bonanza Mine, believed to be the biggest pocket mine ever found in the Mother Lode, was located on Piety Hill, less than 100 yards from St. James Episcopal Church. First worked by Chileans, who took out a large amount of surface gold, it was purchased for a pittance by three partners in the 1870's. After several years of patient work, they broke through into a body of almost solid gold. Within one day they had sent $160,000 worth of gold to the San Francisco mint, and within a week another $500,000 was taken out of the mine.

Sonora was the location of one of the most popular of all Gold Rush Country stories. It concerns a Mexican and his three Indian companions who were found by American miners burning the corpses of two Americans. It took little time once Sonora learned of the act for lynch law to enter the story. But before the proceedings reached the point of no return, the prisoners were rescued just in time by an armed sheriff's posse.

The town was sullen, and rumors spread that a band of guerrillas was stationed outside town waiting to sweep in to rescue the prisoners. The sheriff responded to this by rounding up over a hundred Mexicans, most of whom just arrived in the area, on suspicion of murder. These prisoners were held in a corral to await examination after trial of the Mexican and his Indian friends.

Tension mounted and the town was swollen with hundreds of miners who had come for the trial. Just as court was about to convene, an accidental shot sparked an outbreak of gunplay and only by some miracle was bloodshed averted.

Belly up *to the bar for a cold sarsaparilla at the Stage Driver's Retreat; try some miner's rock crystal at the Candy Kitchen; investigate the Wells Fargo scales; or climb aboard the stagecoach (shotgun seats are extra) for a ride through the hills. These are some of the attractions at Columbia.*

WELLS FARGO SCALES

Shipped around the Horn in 1853, these scales were an in the banking equipme... Wells Fargo's office in Columbia, California. Over the ...ed in" some $50,0... worth of Tuolumne County gol... The old Wells Fargo buil...were used was off... presented by the bank to the ...e Park Commission in J...nor Earl Warren ... the bill designating Columbia ...part of California's Stat... was the initial gif... project which is to preserve and ...store Columbia as a ty...ush town.

The trial began and the miners, whose tempers had been somewhat dampened by the wild outburst of shooting, must have felt even more sheepish — perhaps even ashamed — when the truth about the burning of the bodies was revealed: the Mexican and the three Indians were guilty of nothing more than committing an act of simple charity. They had discovered the murdered bodies of men they had never seen before, and taking time out from their search for gold, had built pyres in accordance with their religious beliefs.

Once the men were freed, the judge turned to examination of the hundred-odd prisoners who had been held in the corral. All were exonerated, and the matter was closed.

On a minor road (Sawmill Flat) east of State 49 between Sonora and Columbia, Squabbletown, Sawmill Flat, and Yankee Hill were located. Once meaningful names to the argonauts, they are now just memories.

Columbia. This was — and still is — one of the most important settlements in the Gold Country. When its mines were producing at a record pace in the 1850's, Columbia was called the "Gem of the Southern Mines." It deserves equally high billing today, not for its gold but for its unparalleled collection of reconstructed buildings and mining artifacts.

Every visitor to the Gold Rush Country should visit Columbia. In fact, it makes a good starting point, because here you can pick up a sizable fund of knowledge about architecture and miners' habits that will help you figure out the sometimes confusing ruins and deserted mining camps located elsewhere.

There is no reason for any first-time visitor to get lost or wonder about the identity of any building. Columbia is maintained as a state historic park, and everything is clearly labeled. In addition, there is an abundance of maps, guide books, and souvenirs that go to great lengths to explain history and current attractions in detail.

Some visitors will be disappointed at Columbia's blatant commercialism, but there is so much to see and do in this one place that it cannot honestly be avoided.

Historically, Columbia ranked as the largest town in the Southern Mines during its heyday. Some 15,000 people lived here when the earth was giving up a fortune, estimated at $87 million. The town rang with the clamor of hectic activity and the shouts and curses of thousands of miners, gamblers, merchants, dance hall girls, and miscellaneous camp followers who always managed to thrive in the most successful camps. Stagecoaches rattled into town every day, and the roads were crowded with freight wagons bringing in new provisions and merchandise from Stockton.

Gold was discovered here in 1850 by Dr. Thad-deus Hildreth. The camp was first named Hil-dreth's Diggings, later American Camp, before being christened formally as Columbia at the time of incorporation in 1852. The town was known for i... energetic citizens, but it also had its share of vi... lence and brutality. In fact it was here that ... shockingly ugly lynching took place.

A townsman named John Huron Smith wea... into a bar owned by Martha Barclay on one ... tober afternoon and called for a drink. Mr. Sm... was in no need of a drink, and in no time an a... ment broke out between him and Martha, a w... an whose personal reputation matched that o... establishment — bad. Her swearing appar... caused Smith to push Martha and slap her in ... Just as he did, Martha's husband, John Bar... appeared at the door, saw what was happe... and in an instant had drawn his pistol and ... his wife's tormentor.

It might have all been forgotten as a justifiable act, but the Barclays' name was unloved and Smith happened to be a good friend of State Senator J. W. Coffroth, an accomplished orator. Coffroth had no intention of letting the matter die, and he succeeded in warming a mob to lynch heat. They stormed the jail where Barclay was held and, overcoming the guard, took the terrified prisoner down the Gold Springs Road to a great flume which towered 40 feet over the crowd. Kangaroo Court was quickly assembled, and it was obvious that only one verdict could be delivered, but before the "jury" returned from their deliberation, the sheriff arrived and attempted to take the prisoner from the mob. The sheriff was swamped by the mob, which then swept Barclay beneath the flume where a hastily-tied noose was put around his neck. The rope was thrown over the flume, and the howling mob watched a dozen men jerk the unfortunate man into the air.

But there were no cheers, for there by flickering torchlight they saw in horror their victim hanging onto the rope above his head — in their frantic rush to have justice, no one had thought to tie his hands.

They quickly jerked the rope up and down, but still Barclay held fast — as long as he could keep the rope slack he would live. Then several of the lynchers clambered up the flume supports to shake the rope, but to no avail. Finally tradition has it, one miner crawled out with a pistol and mercilessly battered Barclay's fists. He dropped, and with a final convulsive kick, died.

Now, more than a century later, Columbia is far removed from her days of violence, but she is still more than a collection of restored buildings. There is still a living community, albeit tourist-oriented. Children can enjoy panning for "color" down in Matelot Gulch, riding the jouncing stagecoach from the Wells Fargo office through the granite-ribbed hills behind town, sipping sarsaparilla at the Stage Driver's Retreat saloon, or getting a haircut at the oldest barber shop in the state. There's Hangtown Fry or some other fortyniner delicacy to sample amidst the turn-of-the-century elegance of the Columbia House Restaurant. Fallon House is still the setting for summer theatricals (see pages 42-43).

Burned out a number of times, including a disastrous blaze in 1854, the rebuilding of Columbia was done with brick, fireproof doors, and iron shutters — one reason for the pretty much intact town. Restorations increase steadily as more state park funds become available.

Probably the first brick church in California, St. Anne's on Kennebec Hill west of town overlooks the world's richest placer grounds where ghost-like rocks left from diggings encroach to the very edge of the little cemetery.

A climb up a hill at Columbia's north end takes you to a two-story schoolhouse, constructed of brick in 1860 and recently restored. This was one of California's earliest public schools.

During the summer you can tour an operating quartz mine on Italian Bar Road. On the campus of the junior college, built around the San Diego Reservoir (once Columbia's water system in Gold Rush days), you can see a gigantic hydraulic basin. Students have built a nature trail down into the sink. You'll pass the hydraulic mining monitor at Knickerbocker Flat on the way to the college.

Informative display at Columbia State Historic Park museum explains the various types of gold deposits.

Hiss the villain, cheer the hero, then mingle with the cast at the local saloon after the performance. You can do so every summer weekend (one company performs year-round) at several theaters throughout California's Mother Lode. Some groups offer comedy or more serious plays, but the majority have old-fashioned melodramas.

Nevada City. Over the years the venerable theater in Nevada City has featured such well-known personalities as Mark Twain and Lola Montez. The century-old building is being restored to former elegance. For program information, write to Old Nevada Theater, 401 Broad Street, Nevada City, California 95959.

Auburn. The Old Opera House in Gold Rush Plaza presents Friday and Saturday night melodramas from June to September. For the summer schedule, write to Old Opera House, 111 Sacramento Street, Auburn, California 95603.

Folsom. The Sutter Gaslighters perform every weekend with shows changing every four months. Tickets are $2.50; performances start at 8:30 P.M. Friday and Saturday. Write to The Sutter Club, 720 Sutter Street, Folsom, California 95630, for show and dinner reservations.

Drytown. The Claypipers, one of the oldest performing groups in the Gold Country, offer polished melodrama and olio productions each Saturday night from Memorial Day through Labor Day weekends. For tickets ($3.50) write to Mrs. Cleo Nokes, Drytown Club, Drytown, California 95699, or call (209) 245-3812.

Mokelumne Hill. Light-hearted comedy performances take place every Saturday night throughout the summer in the Garden Courthouse Theater of the Hotel Leger. Dinner is available to theater-goers. Write to Hotel Leger, P. O. Box 50, Mokelumne Hill, California 95245. Show tickets are $3.

Folsom actress tries to remember wall motto.

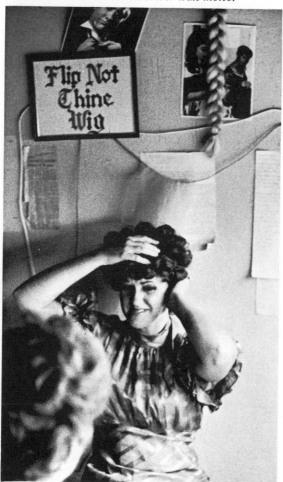

Heroine is in danger at Drytown melodrama.

THE MOTHER LODE

Murphys. Though there are no performances during the summer, the Black Bart Players offer melodramas on April and November weekends. For information and reservations, write to Black Bart Players, P. O. Box 104, Murphys, California 95247. Tickets are $2.

Columbia. The Fallon House Theatre is the setting for the University of the Pacific Repertory Theatre's seven-week season. Beginning the first weekend in July, performances are held Tuesday through Saturday at 8:30 P.M. with a Sunday matinee at 2 P.M. Tickets are $2.50 ($3 on Friday and Saturday) for adults, half-price for children under 12. For information on the program, write Drama Department, University of the Pacific, Stockton, California 95204. For reservations, write to Fallon House Theatre, Columbia State Park, California 95310, after the third weekend in June.

Mariposa. The open-air amphitheater in Mariposa City Park is the setting for melodramas, plays, and movies from July through Labor Day, on Tuesday through Saturday at 8:30 P.M. On weekends, tickets are $1.75 for adults; $1.25 for children under 14. Weekday prices are somewhat less. One tip: Bring a pillow to sit on. For information on the rotating schedule, you can write or phone, (209) 966-2498, the Mariposa County Department of Parks and Recreation.

Oakhurst. At the Oakhurst Community Center, the season begins for a three-melodrama repertory around the middle of July. Performances will be given Friday and Saturday nights through August. Tickets for the cabaret-style theater are $2.50 for adults, $1 for children under 13. For more information on the schedule, write to Golden Chain Theatre, P. O. Box 604, Oakhurst, California 93644 or call (209) 683-7112.

Musicians tune up at Fallon House Theatre.

Springfield. Named for a prodigious spring that gushes forth from between limestone boulders as the source of Mormon Creek, this was one of the best laid out of the mining camps. There was a central plaza, and the town spread out over a square mile.

The only building left on the square is the old brick Methodist church that also served as school and courthouse and was even converted to military use at the beginning of the Civil War.

Near the intersection of Shaws Flat Road and State 49 is the site of a lime kiln where limestone was ground into the powder necessary for mortar in brick and stone buildings.

Shaws Flat. In 1849, Mandeville Shaw planted an orchard on the eastern slope of Table Mountain, and the site became known generally as Shaws Flat. The Mississippi House, built in 1850 as com-bination post office, store, and bar, still stands to-day but is scheduled for demolition. The post office will be rebuilt and put on exhibit at the museum in Sonora. Nothing remains of another bar that stood across the street except one of the Gold Country's best legends.

It was at this bar, it is said, that an enterprising bartender supplemented his daily wages in a particularly imaginative way. It seems that he would drop on the bar a wee bit of each pinch of dust that he took from the miners' pokes for their drinks. Now this took slight imagination, but the ingenious part of the larceny lay in his method of recovery.

Periodically leaving the bar to tramp around in the mud made by a little spring behind the building, he would return to his station and carefully pick up with his muddy boots all the gold dust he had dropped and carefully brushed to the floor.

Along Highway 49 *are many pleasant places to stop and stretch your legs. Meadow,* **above,** *is typical of scenery around Jackass Hill. Nearby is a reconstruction of the cabin once occupied by Mark Twain* **(bottom right).** *Large plaza in Springfield once was ringed by buildings. Today, there is only one decaying structure* **(top right)** *on square.*

Then at night he panned out the mud scraped from his boots — and rich diggings they were. According to the story, he averaged about $30 a night during the week, and several times that on the weekends.

Shaws Flat was the starting place in the career of James Fair who went on to amass a fortune in the Comstock Lode, and there are some who say that it was he who tended bar at that now-vanished saloon across from the Mississippi House.

Another remnant of the mining period is the old bell (now on display at the school house) that once was used to call the men to the mines and meetings.

At the south end of town once stood "Uncle Tom's Cabin," home of a former slave who purchased his freedom with gold he took from the ground. In appreciation for his blessings he kept a pail of clear water outside his door for thirsty wayfarers.

Tuttletown. Today Tuttletown isn't much more than a wide spot in State 49, but it was once a thriving placer-mining area on Mormon Creek. You can still see the ruins of Swerer's store, where Bret Harte was once a clerk and Mark Twain was a customer.

The town was named after Judge Anson A. H. Tuttle, who built the first permanent house in Tuolumne County in 1841.

Jackass Hill. In the midst of a very productive placer-mining area, Jackass Hill got its name from the braying of the hundreds of mules that were tied up here overnight when the pack trains stopped to rest.

Main attraction now is a reconstruction of a cabin where Mark Twain lived for five months as the guest of the Gillis Brothers, who reportedly were hiding in the hills because one had belted a San Francisco bartender with a bottle. While here, Twain wrote about the jumping frog that he heard about in Angels Camp (see page 48). The cabin's site is authentic, and the old stone fireplace is supposed to have survived the fire that destroyed the original cabin.

Rawhide. If the term "rawhide" conjures up visions in your mind of "Wild West" towns and tough hombres, the mining settlement of that name will come as a surprise. This is as quiet an inhabited area as you'll find in the entire Mother Lode. The farms of today give no hint that this was the location of a quartz mine that once was considered one of the world's greatest.

OLD BOTTLES ALMOST WORTH THEIR WEIGHT IN GOLD

There is a modern-day counterpart to the feverish '49er who rushed around the Gold Country in search of that big strike. But it is not the glitter of gold in the gravel that attracts the eye of these twentieth-century prospectors—it is the glitter of glass. The new craze is for antique bottles. Old bottles once worth nothing are now worth their weight in gold.

During the 1950's, only a few people were interested in bottle collecting, and those who had some foresight into the collector's market could go out and dig them up by the dozens or even hundreds. As bottles became more popular and more valuable, there was a new rush of "miners" who wanted a share of the wealth. But the "cream" was gone, and more work was required to get fewer treasures.

If you are interested in old bottles, you should get familiar with the objects of your search. You can find good collections of bottles in many Gold Country shops. John Fountain, owner of an antique bottle shop in Amador City, publishes "The National Bottle Gazette" and some reference books on bottles.

Large collections of old bottles are often divided into seven categories: bitters, whiskey, poison, soda, beer, ink, and pharmacy. In general, there are more pharmacy bottles buried in the ground than all the other categories combined. In the Mother Lode, the two most commonly found empties carry the labels of Lash's Bitters and Dr. J. Hostetter's Stomach Bitters. Almost every old bottle is worth something, but the most valuable containers are those with distinctive color, writing, or other identification. A 120-year-old plain glass bottle without a mark may be worth less than $10, while a 60-year-old blue cobalt beer bottle may sell for $90 and a 20-year-old Royal Ruby decanter $40.

The exact age of a bottle is difficult to determine. But experts can make a pretty good estimate, based on the quality of the glass, the type of seam, and the lip style.

Finding bottles involves a good bit of luck as well as hard work. First you have to find a site. The best burial grounds were old mining towns' garbage dumps. However, much of the Gold Country is now privately owned, so diggers have to worry about the rights of others. There is also some danger involved. Old mine shafts and caves are notoriously weak, and they may collapse at any time.

The key to digging for bottles is patience and very careful spadework. Many of the old bottles are very brittle, and a wayward swipe with a shovel can crack or smash the treasure. Also be careful when cleaning the bottles.

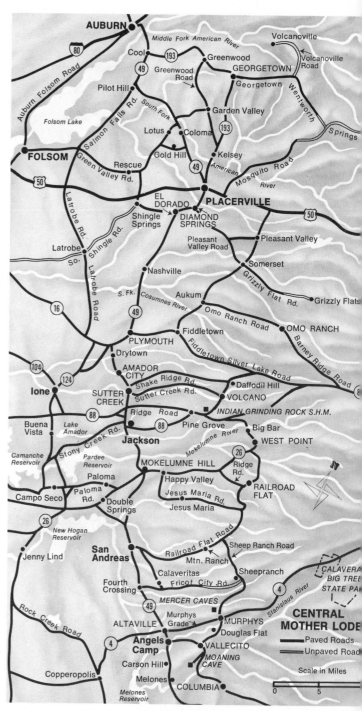

Central section *of Gold Country includes the place where it all began. You can easily find bronze statue of James Marshall (left) at Coloma, pointing to his discovery site. Final resting places of unknown pioneers, like one (right) in little-visited Campo Seco, are harder to locate.*

THE CENTRAL MOTHER LODE

ANGELS CAMP · MURPHYS
SAN ANDREAS · JACKSON
PLACERVILLE · COLOMA

ALTHOUGH MUCH of California's Gold Country was called the Mother Lode, the section between Melones to the south and Auburn to the north contained the primary gold vein that gave the area its name. This region had the deepest, and some of the richest, mines, and although it is the most-visited part of the Gold Country, it retains a surprising number of relatively intact historical towns and buildings.

Travelers will find it easy to locate accommodations, ranging from old inns to new motels. There are some exceptionally good restaurants, although you'll have to ask local people for suggestions as most of them are off State 49.

A large number of the colorful annual events are held in this area, including the crowd-drawing Jumping Frog Contest. There are probably more year-round family recreational activities such as fishing, boating, swimming, and skiing in this section than in any other part of the Gold Country.

THE ANGELS CAMP AREA

Angels Camp, thanks to Mark Twain, is probably better noted for its annual frog-jumping contest than for its Gold Rush background. However, there are some remembrances of the past here — the Angels Hotel, ruins of a mine, a museum, and once-important buildings.

Side trips from Angels Camp take you on state highways and back-country roads. You'll see evidences of mining at Sheepranch (George Hearst ran this mine) and at Carson Hill. Copperopolis was a major copper-producing center when people were craving gold. Murphys claims the oldest continuously-operated elementary school in the state, Altaville the oldest iron foundry in the state.

Other points of interest are Melones Reservoir where you can picnic, camp, or pan for gold; Calaveras Big Trees State Park where you can walk among the *Sequoia gigantea;* and the Mercer Caves and Moaning Cave where you explore limestone caverns.

Angels Camp. This busy little town takes its name from George Angel, a member of the 7th Regiment of New York Volunteers who came west in 1848 and founded a trading post where Angels Creek and Dry Creek come together. The town grew fast during the 1850's, and, although the setting was changed, it was probably the town Bret Harte wrote about in "Luck of Roaring Camp."

The discovery of the quartz lode which was to make Angels Camp one of the greatest mining centers in the Mother Lode is often told this way. A miner named Rasberry, for whom Rasberry Lane —still a public way in Angels Camp—was named, was having difficulty with his muzzle-loading rifle one day. The ramrod had jammed and in a moment of exasperation he fired the rifle into the ground. The ramrod shot out and struck the ground with force. When he went to retrieve the rod, he found a piece of rock which had broken from the impact and glittered with what was unmistakably gold. Rasberry took almost $10,000 from the new claim in three days and went on to make a fortune following the vein.

Among the most notable buildings still to be seen in Angels Camp are the Angels Hotel, where Mark Twain first heard about the jumping frogs, and the imposing jailhouse behind it. At the other end of town is the iron-shuttered, green-and-white Peirano building. The Angels mine, one of the best in the area, was located across from the Catholic church; only the foundations remain.

The museum near the north end of town has good collections of minerals and early-day artifacts. In the yard outside are an old steam engine, a cannon, and a section of one of the world's largest drill cores.

Every May Angels Camp comes alive with the Calaveras County Fair. What really gets the town jumping during this fair are long-legged frogs. In 1928, the city fathers decided to celebrate the paving of the streets in Angels Camp by staging a frog jump, in honor of Mark Twain's famous story,

"The Celebrated Jumping Frog of Calaveras County." The idea was a good one, and the international frog-jumping contest at the Calaveras County Fair has achieved worldwide recognition.

The fair, itself, has all the trappings of most other county fairs. But the frogs give it a special quality. They arrive by the thousands — some contestants bring them from distant and secret points, and others catch them in the marshy land on the fairgrounds. Any frog at least four inches in length from nose to base of tail is eligible to jump, and fame and riches go to the contestant whose frog jumps the farthest in three consecutive jumps. The strange and mystic rites performed by contestants to encourage their entries into Herculean efforts often overshadow the actual performance by the frogs, and the erratic efforts of man and beast add up to a very entertaining show.

The city has erected a monument to the frog along the main street and has placed an imposing statue of Mark Twain in the shady park along State 49.

Angels Camp *"hangs its wash"* **(bottom right)** *on State Highway 49 during the county fair, best known for the Jumping Frog Contest* **(top right)**. *Hoisting equipment from Lightner Mine* **(bottom left)** *is on display near city park. Prince and Garibardi building* **(top left)** *is in Altaville, 1 mile north.*

Along State 49 between Angels Camp and Carson Hill sits a large, lonely stone house that is slowly but steadily falling to pieces. This is the Romaggi home, the only remnant of the town of Albany Flat. James Romaggi arrived from Genoa in 1850; scorning gold, he built this house and planted vineyards and orchards to establish one of the finest ranches in the Mother Lode. The stretch of road on either side of the famous house was lined with buildings. But his luck ran out, a drought killed the vines and trees, and Albany Flat faded from sight. Only this curiously complicated building has survived in the very parched surroundings.

Carson Hill. South of Angels Camp on State 49 is Carson Hill — considered in its heyday to be the richest of all the Mother Lode camps. Many big nuggets were taken from the ground here, including one that was 15 inches long, 6 inches wide, and 4 inches thick. It weighed 195 pounds and was worth about $43,000 in those days, about $73,000 today. The consolidated mines of Carson Hill and Melones produced over $26 million in gold.

The town was named for James Carson, a part-time miner who traveled to the region with George Angel (of Angels Camp) and the Murphy brothers, John and Daniel. There are no buildings of any character left, and the most conspicuous reminder of the mining days is the "glory hole" of the Morgan Mine in the hill above town. Fifteen miles of underground mine workings honeycomb the hill, and one of the shafts reaches down almost 5,000 feet.

Melones. Mexicans who first established this gold camp on the banks of the Stanislaus River near the present crossing of State 49 named it Melones (Spanish for "melons") because the gold they found here resembled melon seeds. Later miners tried to change the name to Slumgullion because of the thick heavy mud which made mining so difficult, but the original name clung even more tenaciously than the mud.

In 1848, John W. Robinson started the first ferry crossing in this area just upstream from Melones. It was a profitable enterprise. During the summer of 1850 alone, he had collected $10,000

Carson Hill (above) *is honeycombed with early mine workings which once produced many millions in gold.* **Romaggi home (top right)** *is all that remains of Albany Flat, situated between Carson Hill and Angels Camp.* **Boaters (bottom right)** *enjoy Stanislaus River at site of old Robinson's Ferry.*

BRET HARTE AND MARK TWAIN—VOICES OF THE WEST

Bret and Mark — famous Gold Rush writers.

Bret Harte and Mark Twain are the most famous and most popular of the many writers who have used the California Gold Rush for inspiration, background, and characters. They were among the first to recognize the unique qualities of the Gold Rush, and their writings did as much to inform the world of this phenomenon as any history book ever could.

Strangely enough, neither man spent much time in the mines. But their brief exposure to the Western frontier had a lasting impression on both men, and they were able to draw on their California experiences for decades to come.

Bret Harte was only 12 years old and living in New York when gold was discovered at Coloma in 1848. He came to California in 1854 to join his mother who had married a San Francisco man after her first husband (and Bret's father) died in 1850. The reunited family settled down in Oakland, but young Bret, yearning for new adventure, started for the foothills.

Harte arrived in the Southern Mines in 1855, when the first flush of the Gold Rush was already over and many of the mining camps were disintegrating. He taught school for a time in La Grange, and then moved on to Robinson's Ferry on the Stanislaus River, where he was welcomed by superstitious miners who believed that a tenderfoot always brought good luck. Harte quickly acquired some partners, and they mined haphazardly for a few weeks, moving as far north as Angels Camp. It is believed he eventually wound up at the cabin on Jackass Hill owned by the Gillis Brothers. Shortly thereafter Bret returned to his stepfather's home and never again returned to the mines.

By his own admission, Bret Harte never really got to know the towns or the people intimately during his short stay in the Gold Rush Country. He was always the dude, wearing boiled shirts and patent leather shoes, and standing away from the intimacies of mining life. He didn't like the Sierra and wrote that the foothills were "hard, ugly, unwashed, vulgar, and lawless."

After his trip to the mines, Harte embarked on a successful career as printer, newspaperman, magazine editor, and writer. His future was assured in 1860 with the publication of *M'liss*, the first of his mining stories.

Harte eventually became the leading man of letters on the Pacific Coast and went East to capitalize on his fame, abandoning California forever. But he never turned his back on the West as a subject for his writing, and many of his best stories — even those written when he was living in England after 1885 — dealt with frontiersmen and life in the mining towns.

Samuel Clemens was born in Missouri in 1835 — a year before Bret Harte — but did not arrive in the West until 1861. By that time, he had served as newspaperman, printer, Mississippi River pilot, and even a Confederate soldier for two weeks at the start of the Civil War. He left the East to accompany his brother Orion, the newly-appointed secretary of the Nevada territory. Young Sam tried prospecting in Humboldt County, Nevada, then worked as city editor of the Virginia City *Enterprise,* where he first used the pseudonym of Mark Twain in 1862.

The young writer moved to San Francisco in 1864, and there met Bret Harte, who was a great help in getting Twain stories published and in improving the author's style.

In December, 1864, Twain visited the Gillis boys who had been kind to Bret Harte a few years earlier. They tried pocket mining for a time and spent a lot of time in Angels Camp during the inclement weather. It was on a cold January day that Twain heard an old Mississippi River pilot named Ben Coon relate a funny anecdote about a frog-jumping contest. A few months later, Twain wrote "The Celebrated Jumping Frog of Calaveras County" and became an overnight literary sensation. The next year, he left California and never returned.

Mark Twain collected enough other material in the mining country to last him for many years. He made a point to learn the miner's habits and his trade. He once said: "I know the mines and miners interiorly as well as Bret Harte knows them exteriorly." There was the major difference between the two. Harte had a genius for the narrative and could capture character and local color in just a few words. But his stories lacked depth and were those of an outsider. Twain, on the other hand, wrote like he talked — with a vitality that more truly reflected the California frontier and the rough people who settled it.

The two voices of the West died within a few years of each other. Twain was in Connecticut when the end came in 1910, and Harte was in England when he died in 1902.

On display *under glass at Old Timers Museum on main street of Murphys are Gold Rush documents.*

Fine exhibit *of period rifles on the wall of a museum in Murphys will delight any gun-fancier.*

for ferrying freight, animals, and miners across the river. The story is told of a circus on its way to Columbia whose owners tried to convince the operator to take their elephant, Lucy, across. Despite a heated argument, he refused. Poor Lucy, attempting to swim, was carried downstream and drowned, whereupon the circus immediately dissolved, and its people joined the ranks of the gold seekers.

Melones now lies underneath a reservoir, and Robinson's Ferry will one day be inundated, with only a plaque and a vista view as a reminder. The ruins of the ferry system may still be seen adjacent to the present bridge. It is a popular place for picnicking, camping, and amateur gold panning.

Vallecito. East of Angels Camp on State Highway 4 sits Vallecito, which means "little valley" in Spanish. It was settled in 1850 by Mexican miners but did not become a prominent camp until a rich strike in 1852. Still standing at the south end of town are the Dinkelspiel store and Wells Fargo Express office. An old miner's bell and town monument are in front of the Union church on the main street. Two miles south of Vallecito is the Moaning Cave (see page 55), a former Indian burial ground.

Douglas Flat. Douglas Flat, a serene little community about 2 miles north of Vallecito on State 4, has preserved only one stone-and-adobe building from its mining days. The Gilleado building once served as the town store and bank. The safe inside was used as a vault for storing large quantities of gold. To be sure that it was adequately protected, an armed guard was stationed here. His "shotgun window" can still be seen beside the rear door.

An interesting story is told about the Douglas Flat School. It is said that because the building was located on gold-bearing gravel, part of the teacher's salary was the right to pan for gold during recess.

Murphys. Tall locust trees line the streets of this grand old town, and in their shade life goes on much as it has through the decades since the Gold Rush died. In its beautiful setting, Murphys is one of the most charming "live" towns in the Mother Lode and an ideal place to take a casual stroll and soak up the atmosphere.

Murphys was first settled in July, 1848, by John and Daniel Murphy, and its rich diggings built the substantial town of brick and limestone buildings that you see today.

Murphys' *one-room jail is located opposite the old hotel. Rumor is the builder was its first occupant.*

The most prominent of the old structures is the famous Murphys Hotel (see pages 58-59), built by James Sperry and John Perry in 1855 to accommodate the growing number of visitors passing through on their way to view the newly-discovered "Big Trees of Calaveras." You can examine the old register and find names of illustrious travelers in the past — Mark Twain, U. S. Grant, Henry Ward Beecher, Thomas Lipton, J. Pierpont Morgan, Horatio Alger, and many others. You might find the entry "Charles Bolton, Silver Mountain"; no one would have taken this quiet traveler for the notorious stagecoach robber, Black Bart (see page 76).

The "Big Trees" are now Calaveras Big Trees State Park. This large stand of *Sequoia gigantea* (about 20 miles northeast of Murphys on State 4) was first seen by John Bidwell while on a scouting expedition in 1841. However, credit for their discovery is usually given to A. T. Dowd, a hunter from Murphys, who brought them to public attention in 1852. Today Calaveras Big Trees State Park offers camping, picnicking, hiking, and swimming and fishing in the North Fork of the Stanislaus River.

Across the street from the Murphys Hotel is an old brick-and-limestone building which was used at the beginning as a bakery and miners' supply store. Farther east is another brick-fronted building with the legend "Stephens Bro's. Cheap Cash" painted across the side. This was, at an earlier time, Jones' Apothecary Shop.

The Peter Traver building, built in 1856, is the oldest building in Murphys, having survived three bad fires. It now houses the Old Timers Museum. The I.O.O.F. Hall, and the Segale, Carley, and Compere buildings all date back to the 1850's and are among other notable old structures. Murphys Elementary School, which was built in 1860, is the oldest continuously-used elementary schoolhouse in California.

St. Patrick's Catholic Church, built in 1858, is considered one of the best examples of early construction techniques. Clay used in the bricks was taken from nearby hills.

Many caverns are found around Murphys. Mercer Caves (1 mile north of Murphys) are developed for visitor exploration (see page 55).

Sheepranch. In this little mountain town north of Murphys on the Sheep Ranch Road, George Hearst, later United States Senator from California and father of the newspaper tycoon, ran the Sheepranch Quartz Mine and helped enhance the great Hearst fortune. It is said that this mine was a profit-maker from the time the first shovelful was dug.

Mountain Ranch. This was the site of an early sawmill, and there are three or four old Gold Rush buildings that are still in good shape. Domenghini's General Store is the oldest building in town. The stone structure across the street, a former fandango hall, now respectably houses a collection of Gold Rush memorabilia.

A monument on the Railroad Flat Road southwest of town marks an attempted stage robbery in 1892 by a lone bandit who pumped buckshot into the stage, killing one girl and wounding the driver and several other passengers. The bandit was never captured.

Altaville. This northern junction of State highways 4 and 49 was first known as Forks in the Road, then Winterton, Cherokee Flat, and finally Altaville. It was settled in 1852 and was a lively little burg during a short period while placer mining held out.

There are a few buildings worth noting. First is the handsome old Prince and Garibardi store, a well-preserved, two-story stone building erected more than a century ago. Close by is the oldest

Art show *in Copperopolis hall was for purpose of raising funds to restore the building. Originally a church, the brick building later became a community center and the town's I.O.O.F. Hall.*

Contestant *at muzzle-loading rifle contest in Mountain Ranch tamps ball, powder, and wadding down his gun.*

iron foundry in California, originally established in 1854 to repair mining machinery and manufacture simple tools.

One of the oldest schools in California can be found on the State Division of Forestry's grounds near Altaville. The brick building was erected in 1858 and served the community until 1950. The walls are crumbling, and there is some talk about tearing it down.

Altaville's name will probably be remembered because it was the starting place of what is today considered by many as the Gold Country's greatest hoax. It was from deep in a mine in nearby Bald Mountain that a human skull — soon to be known to the world as the Pliocene Skull — was taken in 1866 and presented to the scientific world as the remains of a prehistoric man. The argument over authenticity of the skull continued for almost half a century, but it was finally decided that the famous skull actually was Indian in origin and had been placed at the bottom of the mine shaft as an ambitious — and successful — practical joke.

Bret Harte's poem "To the Pliocene Skull," which captures the ridiculous aspects of the whole affair, suggests the horse laughter that must have filled many a miner's cabin. True to the massive scale in which the joke was conceived, no one connected with the "crime" ever revealed his part.

Copperopolis. As its name implies, Copperopolis was one of the few towns in this area that was founded on a mineral other than gold. It was one of the principal copper-producing centers in the United States during the Civil War and boasted a population of several thousand people from 1860 to 1867 when it was producing ore at a record rate.

Strangely enough, the ore was not smelted anywhere near the mine during the early days. It was carried by cart to Stockton, then by river boat to San Francisco Bay, and finally by sailing ship around Cape Horn to New England and Swansea, Wales for processing.

Some of the old buildings in town were built in the 1860's of brick hauled from Columbia, where perfectly good stores were being torn down by miners to get at the gold-rich soil underneath the foundations.

At the south end of town are three notable structures. The biggest — a brick building with huge iron shutters and doors — was once the Federal Armory and served as headquarters for the Copperopolis Blues during the Civil War. Next door are the old warehouse and office buildings of the Copper Consolidated Mining Company. The headframes and waste dumps of the mining operations can be seen across the street. At the other end of town is the I.O.O.F. Hall, originally a church and lately a community center.

Copperopolis is southwest of Altaville via State 4; west of Copperopolis, you will see a long stretch of stone fence along this highway. While there are some vague stories that name Chinese or Chileans as the builders of this fence, the most logical contender for the honors is James Sykes, a resident of now-vanished Telegraph City.

Another vanished community is Hodson, originally located 2 or 3 miles northwest of Copperopolis on Hodson Road. This rich gold-mining town boomed until 1905, and there are numerous remains of the feverish mining activity.

South of Copperopolis, at the crossing of the Stanislaus River, was the site of O'Byrnes Ferry, a famous crossing used by travelers for more than a century. A covered bridge which replaced the ferry in 1862 was removed in 1957 when Tulloch Dam was constructed.

Fourth Crossing. On the banks of Indian Creek, between Altaville and San Andreas, was a rich placer-mining community known as Fourth Crossing — it was the fourth river crossing between Stockton and Murphys. Located just west of State 49, little remains of this once important freight and stage stop.

Lonely wooden structure *in Copperopolis meadow will not be able to withstand elements much longer.*

EXPLORING LIMESTONE CAVERNS

Visitors to the Gold Country have two opportunities to go underground in limestone caves.

Mercer Caves (1 mile north of Murphys) was discovered by Walter Mercer, a miner, in 1885. Looking for water on a hot September day, he sat down in the shade. A force of cold air on his legs led him to the cave entrance, which he excavated and opened to the public in 1887.

Tours take groups through an 800-foot series of galleries, entering at the fissure discovered by Mercer and coming out at an artificial opening farther downhill. The temperature inside is a constant 55°. The limestone has taken such shapes as angels' wings and sea anemones.

Moaning Cave, 2 miles south of Vallecito and about 5 miles from Mercer Caves, was also discovered by miners in 1851. To visit Moaning Cave, you descend 65 feet on wooden stairs, then 100 feet down a spiral steel staircase. The staircase, added in 1922, unfortunately spoiled the acoustics, and Moaning Cave no longer moans.

Indian relics are on display, and an Indian's skeleton lies deep inside the cave. Several strange rock formations have picturesque names.

Both caverns are open daily in summer and on weekends and holidays in winter. There is an admission charge.

BICYCLING IN THE FOOTHILLS

Gold Rush County is not ideal terrain for bicycling — there are too many deep river canyons and steep mountain slopes to encourage casual family outings. But this does not mean that the foothills are completely closed to bicycles. With some advance scouting and careful selection of routes, you can make very pleasant one, two, or three-day trips through scenic mining areas.

Bicycling is a great way to explore the countryside — you get a whole new perspective of the terrain, and you get an idea of the natural obstacles that the miner faced on his travels.

Advance scouting is a good idea. An unplanned sojourn down some road that just "looks good" may well wind up with arduous hill climbing or time-consuming backtracks.

Whenever possible, select routes on the back roads as State Highway 49 is often crowded with vehicles. Don't be afraid to walk your bike — you'll feel much safer walking at the side of the road in heavy traffic than pedaling uncertainly along the shoulder. It isn't always possible to make complete loop trips on Gold Country roads, so you may have to make advance arrangements to be dropped off at the starting point and picked up at the finish.

One of the best single-day runs in the foothills is from Volcano to Sutter Creek. A paved road leads 12 miles through forest and fields on a gentle downhill run that is great for beginners. The creek is beside you all the way — a torrent in spring and barely more than a quiet trickle in late summer. The road is bumpy in spots and narrow, but traffic is usually light. There are many opportunities for picnicking.

Organized bicycle clubs — such as those affiliated with American Youth Hostels, Inc. (AYH) and the Sierra Club — often schedule more rigorous trips. It is not uncommon for these enthusiastic cyclists to cover 30 to 50 miles a day, including some rigorous walking. These organized trips can be rugged for inexperienced cyclists, but seasoned group leaders and careful advance preparations can often ease the pain.

Whether you're traveling in a family group or with one of the organized clubs, plan on carrying most of your own gear. Saddle bags and carriers will hold changes of clothes, personal items, first aid and tool kits, camera, flashlight, maps, and money. Self-sufficiency will serve to increase the feeling of adventure that comes with cycling in the Gold Country.

Calaveritas. A narrow mountain road, roughly parallel to and several miles east of State 49, affords an alternate route between Altaville and San Andreas. Curving Dogtown Road which turns into Calaveritas Road passes through the sites of former mining camps of Dogtown, Calaveritas, Scratch Gulch, and Brandy Flat. Only at Calaveritas is there much tangible evidence of this once flourishing gold area. Formerly a settlement of stores, saloons, and fandango halls (where it was said Joaquin Murieta—see page 27—was a frequent visitor), Calaveritas was destroyed by fire in 1858. A few buildings, including the old Costa store, still stand as mute testimony to a more turbulent time.

IN AND AROUND SAN ANDREAS

Busy San Andreas and sleepy Mokelumne Hill are opposites in appearance today, but both prospered during the same period. Today's reminders of the past in San Andreas are a jail (where Black Bart is said to have slept), a cemetery, a museum,

and century-old buildings. "Mok Hill" has several historic buildings, plus a church and an inn still open for business.

Most of your other exploring in this area is off State 49 where vestiges of the region's golden past can be uncovered by a little searching in the surrounding countryside. There are dredging piles at Jenny Lind; a general store, a cemetery, and a schoolhouse at Campo Seco; and traces of a once-highly productive mine at Paloma. At Rail Road Flat, there is little left to recall its position as a major quartz-mining center.

West Point, which boasts such famous visitors as Kit Carson and Bret Harte, is currently undergoing a new boom — it is now emerging from its past to become a summer residential community.

San Andreas. New highway alignments and other demands of modern civilization have stripped San Andreas of most of its mining camp character and left only a few of the original Gold Rush buildings. The remaining examples of early architecture include the dressed-stone Fricot building that now houses the county library, a two-story I.O.O.F. Hall, and the courthouse which is now home of the Chamber of Commerce and a museum with a

Costa store *in Calaveritas, stocked with Gold Rush memorabilia, is normally closed to all visitors.*

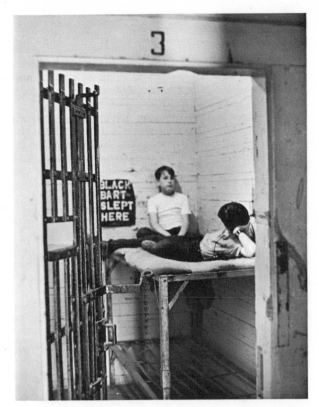

In back of courthouse *in San Andreas is the old jail. This particular cell supposedly housed Black Bart.*

very good collection of local historical items. Behind the courthouse is the old jail with a cell marked prominently "Black Bart slept here."

Just west of town is the historic Pioneer Cemetery, dating back at least to 1851. Most of the graves are unmarked, but the few headstones still standing have some very intriguing inscriptions. Many graves were moved here when Camanche Lake inundated the mining towns of Lancha Plana, Camanche, and Poverty Bar.

A huge cement plant south of town employs many San Andreas residents today. A century ago, the rich gravels yielded gold to the Mexican miners who settled the town in 1849, then to Americans who crowded them out in 1850, and finally to thousands of Chinese who had the patience to rework the tailings considered useless by others.

A minor road, paralleling State 49 on the east side, winds through the foothills between San Andreas and Mokelumne Hill. Only a few evidences of the original character of once important gold camps remain. Poverty Flat, considered by some to be the locale of Bret Harte's "Iliad of Sandy Bar," and Whiskey Slide are only picturesque names. Jesus Maria, marked by a hillside ceme-

tery and a few adobes, was a settlement populated chiefly by Mexicans and named after a farmer who supplied vegetables to early argonauts. Traces of the first vineyard in the area, started by a Frenchman named Frank Dauphin, can still be seen. Fire destroyed Jesus Maria in the late 1800's. Happy Valley, at the junction of State Highway 26 and Jesus Maria Road, is marked by a solid stone building thought to have been a trading post and an old well.

Double Springs. When Calaveras County was formed in 1850, Double Springs was named county seat and kept the honor until the following year.

Double Springs lost its official role under interesting circumstances following a contested election between Mokelumne Hill and Jackson to determine which should be named the new seat (Amador County had not yet been formed). With the issue in doubt, a wagon load of determined young men from Jackson arrived in Double Springs to offer the county clerk there a casual libation. One led to another, so the story goes, and it was an easy matter for the Jackson crew to pack up official paraphernalia and hustle it off to Jackson.

California's Gold Country has several mellow old inns scattered throughout a once-feverish mining area which offer a warm welcome to travelers and serve as bases for exploring the countryside.

Some of the hostelries have been in operation for more than a century and are members of the 100-Year Club; others are historic buildings more recently converted to accommodate guests; one is a replica of a hotel active in Gold Rush times. Accommodations range from rustic to Victorian opulence, but all the innkeepers work hard to preserve the feeling of old-fashioned hospitality.

Reservations are always advisable; some hotels close for brief periods during the year. Half of the inns listed serve meals (although the dining room may close one or two days a week), one serves breakfast only, and others send guests "down the street" for meals.

All the inns listed (in north-to-south order) are in towns on State Highway 49 or a few miles east. Rates quoted are based on double occupancy; meals are extra unless otherwise noted.

Nevada City. National Hotel, Nevada City, California 95959; (916) 265-4551: Gold Rush exterior remains intact and interior furnishings are Victor-

ian; private baths; dining room serves lunch and dinner; pool; '49er Museum; $9 to $22.

Red Castle, 109 Prospect Street, Nevada City, California 95959; (916) 265-5135: Restored 1860-era private residence overlooks city; lovely antiques; suites have private bath; continental breakfast and afternoon tea included; no children; $15 to $25.

Georgetown. Georgetown Hotel, Georgetown, California 95634; (916) 333-4373: Simple Victorian-style rooms; no private baths but 7-foot claw-leg tub is worth the walk; dining room serves lunch and dinner daily except Thursday; $7 to $10.

Coloma. Sierra Nevada House III, P.O. Box 268, Coloma, California 95613; (916) 622-5856: Well-appointed replica of an old-timer; private baths; old soda parlor serves meals and dining also available (with reservations) in Gold Rush and Victorian rooms; $13 includes breakfast.

Amador City. The Mine House, P.O. Box 226, Amador City, California 95601; (209) 267-5900: Formerly Keystone Mine offices; each of 8 rooms (with baths) named for original use —Vault, Retort, Assay, Stores, Grinding, Directors, Book-

Red Castle is haven for antique buffs.

Sutter Creek Inn offers "bed and breakfast."

keeping, and Keystone; morning coffee and juice brought to room; pool; $17.50 to $24.50.

Sutter Creek. Sutter Creek Inn, 75 Main Street, Sutter Creek, California 95685; (209) 267-5606: "About a dozen rooms" in this converted old home; intimate comfort is keynote; some rooms with fireplaces; some have private baths, others share; for fun, try the swinging beds; large breakfast in kitchen or under grape arbor included in price; no children; $17.50 to $25.

Bellotti Inn, 53 Main Street, Sutter Creek, California 95685; (209) 267-5211: Over-a-century three-story hostelry; unpretentious; 28 rooms, 15 with private baths; restaurant open daily for lunch and dinner; $10.

Volcano. St. George Hotel, Volcano, California 95685; (209) 296-4458: Venerable three-story hotel; nearby bathrooms; simple, comfortable furnishings; dining room serves meals with advance reservations; $9 to $12.

Jackson. National Hotel, 2 Water Street, Jackson, California 95642; (209) 223-0500: Old-fashioned saloon entrance; 50 rooms upstairs, over half with private baths; Louisiana House, on lower level,

serves dinner Wednesday through Sunday, lunch on weekends. Many other restaurants close by.

Mokelumne Hill. Hotel Leger, Mokelumne Hill, California 95245; (209) 286-1312: Handsome Victorian hotel; spacious rooms, 7 with private baths; pool; 2 dining rooms open daily (closed Tuesday and Wednesday during winter); $11 to $18.

Murphys. Murphys Hotel, P.O. Box 329, Murphys, California 95247; (209) 728-3454: Two-story 1860-era hotel; 12 rooms upstairs with 2 modern baths (one for women, one for men); 20 motel units with private baths; dining room open daily except Tuesday; historic guest ledger; $8.50 to $21.

Sonora. Gunn House, Sonora, California 95370; (209) 532-3421: Priceless antiques combine with modern conveniences in 1851 adobe hotel, once private residence; 27 large, well-furnished rooms with private baths; $12 to $24.

Coulterville. Jeffery Hotel, Coulterville, California 95311; (209) 878-3400: Originally a store with fandango hall upstairs; 7 rustic rooms; main attraction is Magnolia Room museum and bar adjoining lobby — fine display of all types of currency, rocks, guns, and "sayings."

Sodas are specialties at Sierra Nevada.

Period decor characterizes room in Mine House.

Handsome Hotel Leger has had several facelifts.

Dirty Dog Saloon *on Campo Seco's main street still stands, although very close to disintegration. According to owner of general store across the street, building was originally a butcher shop.*

A Jackson judge was asked to recount the ballots and strangely found that his town had won the county seat.

Today Double Springs consists of the mellow old two-story stone home built by Alexander Reid Wheat in 1860 that has housed seven generations of his family. Behind the house stands a portion of the original courthouse, which was built of camphor wood shipped from China and which at one time housed a courtroom, recorder's office, living quarters for the county clerk, and even a saloon.

The town was named for the two springs which keep a meadow between gently sloping hills green in spring.

Jenny Lind. Once the hub of mining activities on the lower Calaveras River, the town has retreated to a point of sleepy idleness. There are only a few old frame houses, the ever-present I.O.O.F. Hall, and the ruins of an adobe store. About 1902 the first gold dredger operated at Jenny Lind. The many dredging piles still existing give testimony to the gold operations in the area.

The town was founded in 1849 by Dr. John Lind, and there is no evidence that the famous Swedish Nightingale ever came within 2,000 miles of the place. Jenny Lind is located southwest of San Andreas; take State Highway 12 to State 26, continue south to County Road J14.

Campo Seco. This tiny hamlet north of Jenny Lind is not often included on tours of the Gold Country, but it has an unusual number of photogenic ruins. In the center of town is the remainder of the two-story Adams Express building; across the street is a rapidly disintegrating wooden structure called the "Dirty Dog Saloon," although it was originally a butcher shop. The general store is nearly a living museum with some of the original bitters bottles still on the shelves (not for sale), as well as relics of the town's mining days mixed in with more prosaic items like bread and beans.

On a small local road northwest of the center of the village are two rapidly collapsing stone buildings, the only remains of the town's Chinese section. Up on the hill is the white schoolhouse and Protestant cemetery. The Catholic cemetery lies about a half-mile farther west.

FAMILY RECREATION ON FOUR GOLD COUNTRY LAKES

Bring along your fishing pole, bathing suit, water skis, or boat on a visit to the Gold Country as there are many tempting lakes and reservoirs throughout the area. On the west side of State 49 between San Andreas and Jackson (a distance of some 15 miles), there are four lakes that offer a complete range of water activities.

Camanche Lake. Largest of the four lakes is Camanche, on the Mokelumne River. When the dam was completed in 1964, the resulting reservoir inundated the sites of three old mining towns. Although the '49ers are gone, they marked their presence among the cliffs and jagged rocks of the steep gorge upstream from the dam. This area is off limits for speedboating and water-skiing, making it ideal for fishing and slow cruising. It's also a place for sightseeing and hiking to find Miwok Indian caves, complete with grinding rocks, and innumerable mine tunnels, some dug horizontally into the cliffs—all chasing elusive rich veins.

Several bridges were built over the deep gorge in Gold Rush days. Parts of a suspension bridge are still left. Its cables seem out of place, dangling down the sides of cliffs into the water.

Boating is central at Camanche. A "per car" admission is charged at the resort areas (one on the north shore, one at the southern end), with a slight extra fee if you bring your own boat. Rental boats include fishing boats, houseboats, pontoon boats, sailboats, or speedboats. The wide expanse of the west end of the lake is the place for speedboating or water-skiing. You can fish the entire lake for bass, bluegill, catfish, crappie, kokanee, sunfish, and trout.

For extended stays, you'll find campsites, rental cottages, trailer spaces, and all necessary supplies. For information on rates, write to Camanche Lake Park (south shore), P.O. Box 92, Wallace, California 95254; or Camanche Lake North Shore, Route 1, Ione, California 95640.

Into the bank at Camanche Lake to explore tunnel.

To reach the south shore from San Andreas, follow State 12 west about 20 miles; the north shore is 15 miles west of Jackson via State 88.

Pardee Reservoir. Fishing is Pardee's main attraction. The reservoir opens early in the spring, before the beginning of California's trout season. Kokanee fishing is especially good.

Pardee, approximately one-third the size of Camanche, is located upstream on the Mokelumne River and suffers less from summer "drawdown" (release of water) than many reservoirs. This is a fresh-water supply, so swimming and water-skiing are not allowed. Facilities include a swimming pool, launching ramp, boat rentals and private boat berthing, and horseback riding.

You will also find camp and trailer sites, shady picnic areas, and a children's playground. The admission charge covers picnicking.

To get to Pardee, turn west off State 49 in Jackson onto Hoffman Lane (Stony Creek Road) and continue about 10 miles. For further information, write Pardee Marina, Route 1, P. O. Box 224B, Ione, California 95640.

Lake Amador. A few miles north of Pardee is Lake Amador, formed by an earth and rock dam and fed by Jackson Creek. A tiny lake, it has approximately 13 miles of shoreline and a 200-foot-deep main channel. It's large enough to appeal to the serious fisherman and small enough so he doesn't spend too much time locating his "spot." The lake is stocked with many varieties of bass. No water-skiing is allowed.

A large swimming pool atop a hill overlooks the entire lake. At the entrance to the lake is a coffee shop. Your entrance fee includes swimming, fishing, and picnicking. There is an additional charge for boat launching or camping.

From Jackson, take State 88 west to Jackson Valley Road, turn left, and follow the signs through Buena Vista to Lake Amador.

New Hogan Reservoir. Often overlooked by tourists, this reservoir on the Calaveras River offers fishing, boating, swimming, and water-skiing as well as camping and picnic areas along its 50-mile shoreline. There are boat-launching pads on the north side of the rather desolate lake. The fisherman can wend his way upstream for 11 miles to find just the right spot.

There is no admission charge; rental boats and bait are available at the floating marina.

For further information, write Mr. Hi Witt, U. S. Army Corps of Engineers, Valley Springs, California 95252.

To reach New Hogan Reservoir, turn onto State 12 at San Andreas and follow it west to Valley Springs. Turn south and follow the signs for about 3 miles.

Mokelumne Hill *is a favorite with many tourists because of its interesting buildings, some in ruins like the Mayer store* **(top right),** *others restored like the art gallery* **(bottom right).** *The beautiful wooden church* **(top left)** *and three-story I.O.O.F. building* **(bottom left)** *are among the oldest.*

Oddly enough, Campo Seco enjoyed its greatest boom not from the rich placer diggings of the early Gold Rush days, but from the Penn copper mine that opened in the 1860's.

Paloma. At the top of a hill, Paloma was once a large community, but a fire in 1905 destroyed most of the town and it was never rebuilt. Today it is a small collection of undistinguished buildings on a wide place in the road. Behind the local historical marker are the ill-kept remains of a small arrastra which was once used to crush ore.

The fortunes of Paloma rose and fell with the famous Gwin Mine in Lower Rich Gulch, just north of town. William M. Gwin, one of California's first senators, operated the mine for many years. About $7 million was taken out from its beginning in 1883 until it closed in 1908.

The Middle Bar Road takes you down into Lower Rich Gulch past the site of the mine — here you'll see little evidence of the frenetic activity once centered in this narrow ravine. Foundations for a stamp mill and a few terraces on the hillsides are all that remain. Continuing on this road you cross the Mokelumne River at Middle Bar, site of a former gold camp, and return to State 49 just south of Jackson.

Mokelumne Hill. "Mok Hill" is one of the most popular Mother Lode towns because of its winding streets, good collection of early architecture, and unmistakable mountain flavor.

Many of the buildings in Mokelumne Hill are built of light brown stone known as rhyolite tuff, a material common to much of the Mother Lode. Best-known reminders of the Gold Rush are the I.O.O.F. Hall (the first three-story building in the Gold Country), the remains of the Mayer store, and the beautiful wooden Congregational church, built in 1856. The famous old Hotel Leger (still operating as an inn, see pages 58-59) includes the building that once served as the county courthouse. When the county seat was moved to San Andreas, George W. Leger simply made it a part of his adjoining hotel.

The town was started in November, 1848, when hungry miners gave a man named Syree financial backing for a supply depot for the nearby diggings.

In an area that was ridden by violence and international friction, Mokelumne Hill seems to have had more than its share. For instance, tradition has it that there was a stretch of 17 weeks when there was at least one murder every weekend; another time five people were killed in a week.

The diggings were rich in the "Mok Hill" region, so rich in fact that in certain areas claims were limited to 16 square feet. But this wealth didn't keep the Americans busy with their own work all the time. Unlike many other camps which had one "foreign war," Mokelumne Hill had two.

South of town, the now-vanished camp of Chili Gulch was the scene of the "Chilean War" in which Hillites conquered the stubborn Dr. Concha in 1849. But this was not before several men were killed. Here, at least, there was some justification, because Dr. Concha was working his claim with peon labor and had registered claims in the names of men who were slaving for him. Slavery was one universally forbidden practice in the Gold Country.

The "French War," which occurred two years later, was a different matter. French miners who, as a group, had had excellent luck in their mining, raised a French flag above their diggings on a rise, appropriately named French Hill, that overlooks the town. The Americans, using the excuse that the French were defying the American Government, swarmed up the hill and drove the French from their claims. As far as anyone knows, the excuse was hollow — and only envy and greed provoked the incident.

Tall grass *almost hides side of Happy Valley trading post on the Jesus Maria Road near Mokelumne Hill.*

Rail Road Flat. East of State 49 and Mokelumne Hill is this little mountain settlement that was a placer and quartz-mining center for a few years. Far from the nearest railroad, it was named after a few hundred feet of wooden track laid by a miner to carry ore in a mule-pulled car.

Across the road from the historical marker is a grocery store built during the hamlet's early history. In the back part of the building, you can still see the windows and numbered boxes of the first post office in the area (now abandoned).

West Point. Kit Carson came through here early in 1844 searching for a passage over the Sierra. Due to high waters of the Mokelumne River, this was as far west as he could venture — hence the name of the town. A later visitor to West Point was Bret Harte, who lived here for a short time.

Mining was once its main industry with many mills crushing ore, and North Main Street was known in those days as Chinatown. The few old buildings that remain are interspersed with newer ones in the business district.

Big Bar. Where State 49 crosses the Mokelumne River was once the site of one of the most important camps in the 1850's. Here a busy ferry moved miners, gold, and supplies along the Gold Rush highway. When nearby placers gave out, the center of activity moved southwest to the rich diggings in Mokelumne Hill.

Butte City. North of Big Bar, Butte City enjoyed a boisterous but very short life in the 1850's. Once a rival of Jackson, it practically disappeared when mining ended. Today, there is only the badly weathered Ginocchio store, built in 1856, protected by a sturdy fence.

JACKSON AND NORTH

Tangible evidence of some of the largest, and certainly the best known, mines of the Mother Lode are found around Jackson. A lofty water tank of the Argonaut Mine and huge tailing wheels of the Kennedy Mine are still standing on both sides of State 49 about a mile north of town.

There is much to see of Gold Rush days on State 49 north of Jackson. A walk around Sutter Creek takes you by some balconied buildings along the main street and quaint, well-kept houses on the back streets. Amador City has some mining-day remnants, but it is building a reputation for interesting shops where you can browse for antiques or present-day hand-crafted items. At Drytown, you'll see evidences of hydraulicking, plus a post office with a marble floor; Plymouth has some tailings, a museum, and a few old buildings. Around Nashville are headframes and mining dumps left from the first stamp mill in the Mother Lode.

Off the main route are many worthwhile stops. Volcano, east of Jackson, sports a cannon that was ready for action during Civil War days, a jail, and a brewery. North of town is Daffodil Hill, known for its mass of spring color. Ione (west of Jackson), Fiddletown (east of Plymouth), and La-Trobe (northwest of Drytown) have interesting old buildings. One shop in Fiddletown was a Chinese herb doctor's home and store and another was a Chinese gambling house.

This particular area has a number of historic

Majestic foothills *provide dramatic backdrop to stately St. Sava's Serbian Orthodox Church at Jackson.*

Tailing wheel *at Kennedy Mine in Jackson can be reached via footpath. Mine buildings are in background.*

inns — at Jackson, Sutter Creek, Amador City, and Volcano. Other points of interest are the water-powered foundry in Sutter Creek, the D'Agostini Winery east of Plymouth, and Indian Grinding Rock State Historical Monument south of Volcano.

Jackson. Here is one Mother Lode town that has kept up with progress and now shows a modern face to visitors. City planners are striving to preserve some of the Gold Rush feeling, but the demands of twentieth-century commerce keep getting in the way.

The town was first named "Bottileas," a label affixed by Mexican and Chilean miners who were impressed by the abundance of bottles dropped at a spring that served as a watering spot for passing miners. A plaque behind the National Hotel marks the site of the spring.

One of the most interesting buildings in town is the old Brown house, built in the 1860's on a hill about two blocks east of the main part of town. It now serves as one of the county museums. You'll also find the I.O.O.F. Hall and the restored National Hotel, still open for lodging and meals, (see pages 58-59) on the narrow main street. St. Sava's Serbian Orthodox Church, built in 1894, is unusual for its architectural style. This small structure is the mother church for the North American continent.

The most important factor in Jackson's economy for many decades was the large quartz mines surrounding the area. Two of the most important were the Argonaut and Kennedy mines, north of town. They had some of the deepest vertical shafts in the world, extending well over 5,000 feet into the ground.

The Argonaut, easily recognizable today by its lofty water tank, was opened in 1850 and operated continuously between 1893 and 1942. (A restaurant and art center now occupy some of the old mine buildings.) In 1922, 47 men were trapped below the surface by fire in the mine. Frantic rescue operations, lasting for three weeks, were conducted through the connecting tunnels of the Kennedy Mine. When the miners were located, all were dead. A carbide lamp had been used to write a grisly finis: "gas too strong—3 A.M."

The Kennedy Mine started in 1856 and operated sporadically until 1942. Its most famous features are the huge tailing wheels built in 1912 to carry waste gravels away from the mine. They can be seen from State 49, or you can walk up for a closer view by driving out the Jackson Gate Road and taking the well-marked trails. There were two wheels on each side of the road. Only two are standing in their original positions. The others lie in ruins — victims of the elements and age. Plans are now underway for their restoration.

The Chamber of Commerce, at the south end of town, offers "walking tour" maps of each of Amador County's main towns.

Volcano. Northeast of Jackson off State Highway 88 is Volcano, unquestionably one of the most important stops in the Gold Country — not only for what it was in the 1850's but for what it is today.

Volcano's earliest residents were a lively bunch, as intent on developing their little city as they were on digging for gold. Today's residents are also a lively crew, and the community continues to preserve its heritage. Few towns in the Mother Lode have as many things to see and such a tidy setting to see them in.

Volcano is a misnomer. It is true that the town is situated in a natural cup in the mountains, but there is nothing volcanic about the area's mountain structure. Evidently, the settlers just took one casual look around them and settled for first impressions.

Quite a few *old stone corrals still stand throughout the Mother Lode. You'll pass this one in Jackson Valley, west of State Highway 49, by following Stony Creek Road on the way to Pardee Reservoir.*

Jug and Rose *in Volcano offers sourdough pancake brunch on weekends, imaginative sundaes and lunches.*

Misty air *adds atmosphere at Volcano's hillside cemetery where stones relate vain struggles to obtain wealth.*

Gold was first discovered here in 1848 by members of the New York 8th Regiment, Mexican War Volunteers. The first mining camp grew quickly into a city of 5,000 people and was the lively center of a rich mining area that produced some $90 million in gold. When the placer workings gave out, hydraulic mining tore the soil away from the limestone bedrock and sent it funneling through the sluices.

Volcano claims many "firsts" in California's cultural development: first public library, first literary and debating society, first astronomical observatory, first "little theatre" movement. It also had an abundance of saloons and fandango halls to fill the miners' idle hours. At one time, there were three dozen saloons and three breweries. One of the crumbling stone buildings still standing on the west side of the main street housed two separately operated bars.

There are many other remains of the early town —the old jail, a brewery built in 1856, the I.O.O.F.-Masonic Hall, the Adams Express office, the Lavezzo building that once served as a wine shop, the old St. George Hotel (see pages 58-59), and others. The assay office still stands although it was badly burned by a fire in 1971. All are marked for your convenience.

Perhaps the most unusual reminder of Volcano's past is "Old Abe," the cannon that helped to win the Civil War without ever firing a shot.

Volcano's Union volunteers wheeled out "Old Abe" to put down a threatened Confederate uprising. Control of Volcano might have meant that the area's gold would be diverted to the Southern cause. The story is told that in the absence of iron cannon balls, Union men gathered round, river-smoothed stones. "Old Abe" won the battle without firing a shot — its mere presence squelched the uprising.

Volcano's nearest neighbor of any size is Jackson, and during the 1850's the two towns had a sporting rivalry typical of the times. Once a man from Jackson caused quite a stir in Volcano, so reported a Jackson paper at the time, when he produced a $10 gold piece to pay his hotel bill and buy the house a round of drinks. The editor implied that it had been so long since anyone in Volcano had seen a $10 piece that they gathered around the Jacksonian with great curiosity and admiration.

It took only a week for the editor in Volcano to straighten Jackson around. It wasn't curiosity or admiration of the gold piece, it seems, it was Volcano's awe that anyone from Jackson should have that much cash in the first place, and further that he would use it to buy someone else a drink and to pay his hotel bill before slipping out of town.

Just south of town, on the Volcano-Pine Grove Road, are limestone caves where the area's first Masons held their meetings. They are well marked and open to the public.

Three miles northeast of Volcano is Daffodil Hill, famous for its acres of bulbs — all in bloom during the early part of spring.

Buena Vista. Nine miles west of Jackson, at the intersection of the Ione-Buena Vista Road and the Jackson Valley Road, a few buildings mark the site of the old settlement of Buena Vista. An interesting story is told about the old stone store. It was originally built in Lancha Plana, 6 miles away, by William Cook. When the miners moved on to richer fields, the Chinese came to Lancha Plana to scavenge through the tailings. The only virgin ground was under Cook's store. The owner wanted to move his business to thriving Buena Vista and the Chinese craved the land, so a unique bargain was struck. They might have the land gratis if they would move the store and erect it in Buena Vista. Within several weeks the building was taken down, stone by stone, and rebuilt at the crossroads where it has been standing for over a century. It's not really known if the land was worth the back-breaking effort.

Ione. This little town, north of Buena Vista on State Highway 104, has been part of the Gold Country since the earliest days of the Gold Rush, not as a mining camp but as a stage stop, agricultural center, rail center, and clay and sand producer. The Dosch Pit, worked since 1864, is the oldest continuously active clay mine in the state.

Like so many other towns that started as temporary camps, Ione's dignified name (she was the heroine of *The Last Days of Pompeii*) was chosen only after the townsfolk grew embarrassed about "Freezeout" which had been preceded by "Bedbug." The first two may have been accurate, but they did little for civic pride.

Among the city's old buildings are the D. Stewart Co. store, a brick structure erected in 1856, and the Methodist church (1866), a fine example of Gothic architecture. The brooding castle-like buildings on top of the hill are the now abandoned Preston School of Industry, established in 1889.

North of Ione were several lively gold camps, of which nothing remains except for tales of rich strikes. Muletown, a one-time community of several hundred Irish inhabitants, was known more for its citizens than its wealth. Most of them owned horses and were not skilled riders. It is said they could be distinguished miles away "by their flopping limbs and furious riding."

On the south side of State 88 between Ione and Jackson are the headframes and tailings of the once active Newton Copper Mine.

Sutter Creek. Sutter Creek (or "Crick" as it is often called) is named for John Sutter (see page 80), who camped here in 1848 with a group of Indians. The town actually got started when a few of the early miners erected a community tent to use on rainy Sundays when they couldn't get to Jackson or Drytown. It later achieved permanency as an important supply center for the quartz mines that started up in the area in the 1850's. Hetty Green, at one time the richest woman in

WATCHING A FOUNDRY AT WORK

Visitors are welcome during weekday working hours at Knights Foundry in Sutter Creek. If you drop by around noon on Friday, you can watch as molten metal is poured into casts similar to the way it was done almost a century ago.

Knights is the only water-powered foundry in the United States. In continuous operation since 1873 when quartz mining started in the Mother Lode, the foundry designed and manufactured water wheels and other machinery for stamp mills in California, Nevada, Arizona, and Utah. The foundry's own machinery is still quietly run by the original 42-inch water wheel.

Now designated an historical landmark, the old foundry at 13 Eureka Street manufactures drill presses, metal wheels, and machinery for customers as far away as Alaska and Arabia.

Come around Friday noon to watch them pour.

the world because of her Wall Street financial genius, once owned the Old Eureka Mine, located at the foot of State 49's sweeping curve as it approaches Sutter Creek from the south. Tailings and a few timbers are all that's left of the mine.

The town's main street is lined with old buildings, many with balconies. Among the oldest structures are the Masonic and I.O.O.F. halls (1865), Methodist church (1862), Malatesta building (1860), stone Brignole building (1859), and Bellotti Inn (1860), originally the American Exchange Hotel (see pages 58-59). All of the buildings are marked, and many include amusing anecdotes of early-day events.

Many charming residences with a flavor of New England are found at each end of town and along the side streets. One of the oldest, former home of California Senator E. C. Voorhies, is now the picturesque Sutter Creek Inn (see pages 58-59).

One of Sutter Creek's most famous success stories concerns Leland Stanford. As a young man, Stanford acquired some means as a merchant in Sacramento and picked up a stake in Sutter Creek's Lincoln Mine as payment of a merchant's debt. He worked the claim but suffered repeated failures. Discouraged, Stanford decided to sell the property for $5,000 but was talked out of it at the last minute by Robert Downs, the mine foreman. Not long after, a big strike was made and the Lincoln, or Union, Mine became a bonanza. With this money as a start, Stanford became a railroad king, became a U. S. Senator, Governor of California, and founder of Stanford University. The Downs' home is located on Spanish Street, across from the Catholic church, and the mine site is at the north end of town.

Amador City. Jose Maria Amador, a ranchero from what is now the San Ramon Valley, gave his name

Downs house, *in Sutter Creek, was once the home of the foreman of the Lincoln Mine, owned at one time by Leland Stanford. It is said Stanford stayed in cottage in side yard on infrequent visits.*

to this little town and the county that was separated from Calaveras County in 1854. The first quartz discovery in the county was made here by a Baptist preacher. Because of his association with several other men of the cloth, the strike was known as "Ministers' Claim." Quartz mining provided the economic base for Amador City, and the headframe of the very rich Keystone Mine can be seen on the eastern slope above the south end of town. The Mine House (see pages 58-59) is located in the original Keystone Consolidated Mining Company's brick buildings.

State 49 passes through the middle of Amador City, and you'll have no trouble locating the old Imperial Hotel (now divided into shops), the restored Amador Hotel, and a local museum.

Amador City is almost deserted during the week, but because it is becoming so well known for its quaint shops, parking is at a premium on summer weekends.

A side road, paralleling State 49, between Amador City and Drytown, passes through the sites of Bunker Hill, New Philadelphia, and New Chicago. Little of historic interest remains except for a few foundations and remnants of stone walls.

Drytown. Founded in 1848, Drytown is the oldest town in Amador County. From its name, you might guess that it had been settled by men of abstemious habit. But the town actually supported 26 saloons in its prime, and temperance was not a widespread virtue. Dry Creek was the source of the title.

The placer diggings gave out in 1857, and a fire soon leveled the old town. However, several of the

Driving through *the Mother Lode in spring you'll notice wildflowers in bloom alongside road (***above** *at Amador City). You may have to ford a creek (***top right)** *but probably won't disturb any gold panners; and on some back roads, like the one to Latrobe (***bottom right),** *cattle have the right of way.*

old brick buildings, dating from 1851, still stand along the highway. The marble floors of the present post office may be a little cracked, but that probably happened when the marble was hauled here in 1850 by mule team from the Fiddletown quarry, some 10 miles away.

Two miles east of Drytown, on the side road between Drytown and Amador City, is the site of Lower Rancheria, a predominantly Mexican and Chilean mining camp, dating back to 1848. A series of robberies and murders were perpetrated here on the night of August 6, 1855 by a gang of 12 Mexican horsemen. As a result of the tragedy, miners arose en masse and demanded that every Mexican be disarmed and driven from the region. Tempers eventually cooled, but not until much injustice had been done.

A monument marking the mass grave of the Dyman family, killed in the massacre, can be reached by a side road from Amador City. It is on a hill to the right of Rancheria Creek, about a quarter of a mile from the road.

A drive west on State Highway 16, north of Drytown, will show much evidence of the extensive hydraulic mining that was carried on in this area in the late 1800's. Michigan Bar, one of the most prominent of the early gold camps near the Cosumnes River, was washed out by the hydraulicking and is now remembered only by a historical marker along the roadside. Around 1,500 people lived here in the early 1850's.

Latrobe. A country road, west of State 49, passes through the tiny hamlet of Latrobe (take State Highway 16 west to the Latrobe Road and turn north). From 1864 to 1865 it was a way station for a vast stream of commerce over the Placerville-Sacramento Valley Railroad. Now it has reverted to a farming community. A few of the old buildings, including the I.O.O.F. Hall, still stand.

Plymouth. During the 1850's, the settlements of Plymouth and Pokerville grew up side by side on a dry flat. Plymouth has managed to survive as an agricultural center, but Pokerville has vanished except for one old brick-and-stone building.

There is very little in Plymouth to remind you of the Gold Rush. The headframe and tailings from the Plymouth Consolidated mines, which produced over $13 million in gold, are still very evident. The most notable structure in town, the Empire building, was the old mining company's brick office. It is on the main street between the bank and the old Roos building.

An Agricultural Historical Museum, on the fairgrounds, is now open to the public only at the

CAMPING NEXT TO MIWOK MORTARS

Indian Grinding Rock State Historical Monument, a 40-acre park southwest of Volcano on the Pine Grove road, has within its boundaries the largest bedrock mortar ever found in the western United States.

The 7,700-square-foot limestone outcropping has 1,158 mortar holes and 363 petroglyph designs. Because of its geological and historical interest, a replica of the famed rock is on exhibit at the Smithsonian Institution in Washington, D.C.

Before the Gold Rush, Miwok Indians met here in the fall when the acorns were ripe. Using the rock and stone pestles as kitchen utensils, they ground nuts, berries, and seeds into palatable food. From the middens and artifacts discovered, it is surmised that many Indians lived here all year.

Since acquisition by the state in 1968, the park has been developed for year-round day use and overnight camping. From the parking lot an easy 260-yard trail leads across a meadow to the grinding rock, now fenced to prevent further abrasion and chipping

There is a small fee for camping.

Rain collects in mortar holes of grinding rock.

Tiny Fiddletown *observes annual Homecoming cele-bration in May—fiddling contest is the main event.*

Pokerville's *lone Gold Rush building has brick front and back, stone sides; it was once a Chinese store.*

time of the county fair in August, but plans are underway to display the exhibits year-round.

Fiddletown. About 6 miles east from State 49 at Plymouth lies Fiddletown, a sleepy, tree-shaded village in the center of a prosperous dry farming belt that is still worked in many cases by descendants of the pioneers who settled here in the 1850's.

During the Gold Rush, Fiddletown was a sprawling collection of shacks and miners' tents and boasted the largest Chinese settlement in California outside of San Francisco.

Although there aren't too many of the original buildings left in Fiddletown, the flavor of the early days is preserved by a few old structures all within a couple of blocks. The rammed earth adobe at the foot of Main Street was once a Chinese herb doctor's home and store. One of two such structures in the state, it served as the model for the one reconstructed in Coloma's state park. Open occasionally, it still contains much of the paraphernalia of the doctor's trade.

The building across the street, also built in the early 1850's, was once a Chinese gambling house. Up the street is the town's only antique shop, The Forge, originally a blacksmith shop. One of the best preserved buildings is the Schallhorne Blacksmith and Wagon Shop built in 1870.

Fiddletown's fame must, in part, rest on its name. Founded by Missourians in 1849, it was named by an elder in the group who described the younger men as "always fiddling." It kept the

name for almost 30 years, but in 1878 the name was changed to Oleta by the state legislature. This was done at the insistence of Judge Purinton, so the story goes, who had become known in Sacramento and San Francisco, much to his embarrassment, as the "Man from Fiddletown." The old name, whose charm was quickly recognized by Bret Harte and immortalized by him in "An Episode in Fiddletown," was restored in the 1920's.

It was here that a certain Judge Yates reached the limit of his patience in listening to an outlandish whopper and created a classic in courtroom procedure. He heard all he could stand before he finally turned to the witness, banged down his gavel, and said, "I declare court adjourned. This man is a damned liar. Court in session."

The Wells Fargo Company once had $10,000 stolen from their safe. A mob quickly assembled to hang the supposedly guilty party. They strung their man up several times but sympathizers kept cutting him down. He protested his innocence but no one listened until the deputy sheriff and a doctor arrived on the scene. They cut him down and revived him, but he was paralyzed for months. It was later discovered that their victim had not even been in town the night of the robbery, and it was also proven that one of the members of the hanging mob was the actual culprit.

Nashville. Originally called Quartzburg, this area north of Plymouth was one of the earliest quartz-mining districts in the state. The first stamp mill

THE SHOPPING IS GOOD IN AMADOR COUNTY

Shopping is a particular pleasure in the little towns of Amador City, Sutter Creek, Jackson, and Volcano. Small uncrowded shops with picturesque names like Pinchpenny, Early Attic, Odd Ball, and The Shop offer interesting and unusual gifts.

In addition to gleaming antique furniture, china, glass, and silver, you'll find handmade items such as candles, jewelry, pot holders, pottery, and woven scarves, shawls, and wall hangings. Many stores carry old books and posters. The Bandstand Book Shop in Volcano specializes in California history. Two art galleries have oils and water colors, many depicting the surrounding area. Toby Tyler's Gallery publishes *A Stroller's Guide to Sutter Creek* ($1.50) which will enhance your visit with touches of history.

At Christmas time, merchants in these communities make a special effort to recapture the old-fashioned spirit of the season. The scent of freshly-cut pine boughs decorating store fronts pervades the air. Christmas trees glow with candles, and antique ornaments brighten shop windows. Crisp weather is conducive to the cup of mulled wine offered in one store.

Located within a few miles of each other, all four towns could be visited in a one-day outing, but part of the fun is the opportunity to stay in one of the charming old inns, enjoy a meal in some of the restaurants, and taste-test some vintages at the Amador Winery.

For a partial listing of stores, write to the Amador County Chamber of Commerce, P. O. Box 596, Jackson, California 95642.

Bargains can be found in Amador City.

Which bottle is best buy?

Trying it is as much fun as buying it.

in the whole Mother Lode, made in Cincinnati and brought around the Horn from the East Coast, was used at the old Tennessee Mine. Headframes and a mining dump can still be seen from State 49.

PLACERVILLE AND NEARBY

Just north of Placerville on State 49 is Coloma, birthplace of California's golden history. Now a state park, Coloma is one of your most important stops in the entire Mother Lode. In addition to seeing Sutter's Mill, James Marshall's cabin, a statue of Marshall, and miscellaneous buildings, you can picnic or hike along the American River.

Placerville, second largest of all Gold Rush towns along State 49, started as a gold camp and then went on to achieve status because of its location. It was a supply center for mining camps

nearby, a stopping place for miners on their way north and south, a station on the Pony Express route, and a stop on the way to Nevada and silver. Evidence of the Gold Rush is still seen in Placerville in the surrounding cliffs cut away from hydraulic mining.

South, west, and north of Placerville on back roads, you'll find some ruins and relics of the once active mining days in the small but still-surviving towns.

Placerville. One of the first camps settled in 1848 by miners who branched out from Coloma was Dry Diggin's, so called because of the scarcity of water to wash the gold-laden soils. Three prospectors —Daylor, Sheldon, and McCoon — made the first strike and took $17,000 in gold in one week.

The news spread quickly, and Dry Diggin's rapidly became one of the most prosperous camps in the Mother Lode and one of the most important towns in the Sierra Nevada. Its name was changed

Impressive ruin *was once Zeisz brewery, one of Placerville's oldest business establishments. Building was constructed in 1852 of native stone. Entrance, second-story windows are still intact.*

to Hangtown in 1849 after a series of grisly lynchings, and finally to Placerville in 1854 to satisfy self-conscious pride.

Hangtown certainly was not a misnomer. There are several on record, the first of which was actually a triple hanging. Two Mexicans and a white man were accused of robbing a Frenchman named Caillous of 50 ounces of gold dust and were strung up after only a single night's deliberation. "Irish Dick" Crone was another who felt the hangman's noose after he knifed a man to death over a turn of the cards in a game of monte. Two Frenchmen and a Chilean were set swinging for a crime that no one can seem to remember.

But despite this, Hangtown was quick to establish itself as a key point in California history, and one of the most populous of the early mining centers. Even when the gold supply began to diminish, the town remained an important stop on the route between the Northern and Southern mines, a station on the routes of the Pony Express and Overland Mail, and a supply center for other mining camps. Its greatest period of stable growth actually came after the California Gold Rush was over. When the Comstock Lode was discovered in Nevada, the Placerville Road became the main route across the mountains for miners eager to abandon the fading gold for the promise of silver.

Mark Twain tells a humorous story of Horace Greeley's stage ride over the Placerville Road in *Roughing It.* Supposedly Hank Monk (one of the most famous of the stage drivers) said "Keep your seat, Horace, and I'll get you there on time!" Twain goes on to add "and you bet you he did, too, what was left of him!" Judging from Greeley's own description of the jolting ride, the story was not exaggerated.

One of Placerville's famous citizens was J. M. Studebaker, a wheelwright who stuck to his trade instead of mining. From 1853 to 1858 Studebaker made wheelbarrows for the miners at his shop at 543 Main Street (a plaque marks the location). With about $8,000 in savings he returned to South Bend, Indiana, and he and his brothers built what became the largest pioneer wagon factory in the world, which later served as the foundation for the Studebaker Corporation.

Two other well-known Placerville citizens were Phillip Armour, who ran a butcher shop, and Mark Hopkins, who was a grocer in the town's Gold Rush days.

Although most of old Placerville has been modernized, the street pattern is still based on the trails marked off by the miners' pack mules. And if you look at the stores from the rear, away from the glitter of new façades, you can feel the town's age. At Placerville City Cemetery, on Chamberlain Street, tombstones date back to the early 1850's. Poet Edwin Markham is buried here.

There are some old buildings left in the main business district. The Pony Express building on Sacramento Street, just off Main Street, originally was a harness shop when first built in 1858. A Pony Express historical marker can be found in the alley behind the building. The old City Hall was built in 1857, and the building next door was built in 1862 from funds accumulated by Immigrant Jane Stuart who drove a herd of horses across the plains and then sold them. A rock building on the south side of Main Street dates from 1852 and was one of the few structures to withstand the great fire of 1856 that destroyed almost all of the old Hangtown. The I.O.O.F. Hall has been in use since 1859.

The Raffles Hotel (300 Main Street) occupies

Youngsters emerging *from Gold Bug Mine tunnel at Bedford Park in Placerville stop to examine ore car.*

BLACK BART—MOST FAMOUS STAGE ROBBER OF ALL

Highwayman Bart was also mild Charles Boles.

Black Bart arrived in California almost two decades after the '49ers, but he was such a fascinating character that it's hard to leave him out of any Gold Rush history.

Black Bart was, without doubt, the most famous of all stagecoach robbers — and with good reason. He was credited with 28 robberies between 1877 and 1883, and stage drivers throughout northern California lived in dread of the day when Bart would step out of the brush in some secluded ravine and call out politely, "Will you please throw down your treasure box, sir?"

Bart's character and habits were just as interesting as his success. His working clothes were unique. He dressed in a long linen duster and wore a flour sack over his head with holes cut out for the eyes. He was always on foot and carried only a shotgun and a blanket roll in which was tucked an old axe that he used to break open the strongboxes. Bart chose his locations carefully, and always waited for the stagecoaches at sharp bends in the road where the horses would be moving at a walk.

Bart was gentle with his victims and never harmed driver or passengers. It was revealed later that he never owned a single shell for his shotgun and could not have fired it even in self-defense. Bart earned the reputation as a poet by leaving bits of doggerel at the scenes of two early robberies. He signed the poetry as "Black Bart, the PO8 (po-ate)."

This colorful career came to an end when Bart was wounded while escaping from a holdup near Copperopolis, and accidentally dropped a handkerchief with the laundry mark "FX07." The mark was traced to a customer of a San Francisco laundry, and police made one of the most surprising arrests in the city's history. Black Bart, the highwayman, turned out to be Charles E. Bolton, one of San Francisco's leading citizens and a man with close connections in the police department.

After his arrest, Bolton confessed to the crimes of Black Bart and told a strange tale of his life as a westernized Jekyll and Hyde. He was born in Illinois as Charles E. Boles and grew up as an intelligent, well-educated citizen. After serving in the Civil War, he emigrated to California in search of gold. Unable to find any legally, Boles decided to try his hand at highwaymanship.

He worked for a time clerking in several stage offices and studied shipments and schedules. Then in August, 1877, he transformed himself into Black Bart and made his first holdup, on the Point Arena-Duncan's Mill stage along the Russian River. His prior knowledge of stage lines and drivers made the job easy. So he tried it again, this time on the Quincy-Oroville stage. Again, all went smoothly. With success came prosperity. Boles moved to San Francisco, took the name of Charles Bolton, and quickly built a reputation as a non-smoking, non-drinking, God-fearing man with big business interests in the mines. He was seen frequently in prominent social circles, always nattily dressed and wearing fancy jewelry.

Whenever more cash was needed to support this high life, Boles-Bolton-Bart would put away his derby and cane and pack up his linen duster and shotgun. Off he would go to the foothills, knock over a convenient stage, and return to more champagne and jeweled pinkies.

Black Bart's fascinating life did not end with his arrest. During his trial in San Andreas, the newspapers made him a legend by distorting his exploits, ballooning the size of his ill-gotten gains, and grossly exaggerating his talent at PO-8-try. Amid much publicity, Bart was convicted and sentenced to six years at San Quentin. He served his sentence, with some time off for good behavior, and was released.

For a while, Bart stayed around San Francisco. But early in 1888, he left for the San Joaquin Valley where he quietly disappeared into the dusty heat. The last verified report found him in Visalia and moving.

For a time, there was a rumor that Wells Fargo had pensioned the old man and sent him away after he agreed not to rob any more stages. This, too, is in the realm of legend, and no one will ever know for sure just what finally happened to the honorable Charles E. Boles of Illinois, the most famous stage robber of them all.

Marker *in front of this well-preserved native stone building describes it as Shingle Springs' original shingle mill. Other sources insist it was a store, built at a somewhat later date.*

the site of the former Cary House, where Mark Twain once lodged and where Horace Greeley delivered an address to the miners in 1859. Site of the Hangman's Tree is close by. The old Hangtown bell, used to call out the Vigilantes as well as volunteer firemen, now stands at the intersection of Bedford and Main streets.

There is a story told about a broken flag pole that stood on Main Street in 1853. A young army officer had quartered his troops near town and became a frequent off-hours visitor to the city's numerous saloons. This flag pole was later named in honor of Ulysses S. Grant, commemorating his use of it to maintain his balance after a night on the town.

You can visit Big Cut, one of the area's richest ore deposits, by following Big Cut Road southeast of town. At the top of the hill, you can see how the hydraulic nozzles cut away the cliffs. A million

dollars in gold reputedly was taken from a single acre of this rich hill. Mining continued until 1900.

In Bedford Park, 1 mile north of town, the city recently opened the old Gold Bug Mine to visitors. You can don a hard hat and walk into the two shafts, check out a gold pan and sift the sands of Little Big Creek, and drive up the hill to view the stamp press mill. This whole area was once the scene of feverish mining activity. Bedford Park also offers picnicking facilities and has several hiking trails.

Diamond Springs. This was a stop on the Carson Emigrant Trail that mushroomed with the Gold Rush. It was one of the richest spots in the Placerville area, and the population once hit 1,500. But now, with the gold gone and the traffic rerouted, Diamond Springs just sits there in the sun without causing much of a stir.

You'll find the I.O.O.F. Hall — a grand old

Marshall Gold Discovery *State Historical Park can easily take a day to visit. You'll want to see Marshall's cabin* **(top right)**, *a replica of Sutter's sawmill* **(bottom right)**, *and the famed American River behind the mill* **(top left)**. *Children will enjoy examining the old jail cell* **(bottom left)**.

frame building built in 1852 on a foundation of brick and dressed stone — on a hill north of the main street, and one or two other relics that are slowly crumbling away.

El Dorado. Only a few stone relics of the Gold Rush days remain in this faded little community, known as Mud Springs when it was the center of rich placer diggings. Actually, the town was another stop on the Carson Emigrant Trail, but it was not named and incorporated until the miners arrived in 1849 and 1850.

The Wells Fargo Express office is now Poor Red's, a local restaurant. Murals on the inside walls depict the main street of town as it appeared in the 1850's.

Shingle Springs. By-passed by the present U.S. Highway 50, today Shingle Springs is much more interested in serving the occasional motorist than preserving an air of antiquity. A marker on the fine old native stone building at the west end of town designates it as the original shingle mill, al-

though there is considerable disagreement over this fact. Several other structures are being restored and converted into small shops.

The town was named for the cool spring that flowed near a shingle mill built in 1849. Mining started in 1850, and surrounding gulches were dotted with cabins, a few of which still brave the element of time.

Rescue. Originally the site of the Green Valley Ranch in 1850, Rescue later served as a remount station for the Overland Pony Express. Now it is a picturesque collection of buildings dating back to the early 1800's when Rescue was primarily a stage stop. A few tables in a small park make it an attractive picnic stop.

Nearby is Jayhawk Cemetery, more than one-hundred years old.

Gold Hill. On the summit of a hill 7 miles northwest of Placerville are the ruins of the old town of Gold Hill. Roofless walls of a sandstone building bearing the date 1859 mark the site of this one-time mining camp. After the first flush of mining had subsided, Japanese emigrants started the Wakamatsu Tea and Silk Farm Colony in 1869, but the venture failed in two years.

Coloma. This is where it all began. On a cold January morning in 1848, James Marshall (see page 84) picked up a few flakes of gold in the millrace of John Sutter's sawmill (see page 80) and started the Gold Rush that changed the history of a nation and the economy of a whole planet.

Naturally, Coloma was the first of the mining boom towns. By summer of 1848, there were 2,000 miners living on the banks of the river, and the population swelled to 10,000 during the next year. Virtually all of the new miners in the foothills started out at Coloma before branching out to the newer strikes. It was here that Gold Rush inflation hit the hardest. Picks and shovels sold for $50 each, and foodstuffs went for astronomical prices.

This may have been the first boom town, but it certainly wasn't the longest lived. By 1852, there wasn't much gold left and a good part of the population moved on to more golden pastures.

On the grisly side, Coloma was the scene of one of the Gold Country's most celebrated double hangings in 1855.

The principals were Mickey Free and Dr. Crane. Mickey Free was a badman — a robber and a murderer the law had finally caught up with in Placerville. Dr. Crane, a teacher, had been convicted of dispatching one of his pupils, a young

THE CONTRADICTORY MR. JOHN SUTTER

The discovery of gold in Coloma gave John Sutter a golden opportunity to become one of the greatest men in California history. Instead, it ruined him. By 1852, he had lost all of the land and prestige that had taken years to develop, and he had to leave California a bankrupt and broken man.

Sutter's career is full of contradictions. In many ways, he was one of the most appealing of the California pioneers, and his settling of the interior valley was one of the most important milestones in the state's history. On the other hand, many aspects of his personal life are appalling, and most of his problems were the direct result of his own irresponsibility.

John August Sutter was born Johann Augustus Suter in Switzerland in 1803. He married at the age of 23, fathered a family, ran up a tremendous list of debts, and was able to avoid debtors' prison only by abandoning his family and escaping to America. Sutter spent five years traveling through the West and building a fraudulent reputation as a military captain and a man of means, and then set out for California via Oregon, Alaska, and Hawaii. He arrived in Monterey in 1839 and boldly announced plans to establish a great colony.

Sutter picked a spot for his colony where the American River joined the Sacramento. He cleared land, planted orchards and crops, started livestock herds, and pushed back the wilderness. He named his empire New Helvetia, after the ancient title of his fatherland.

In 1841, Sutter bought Fort Ross from the Russians in an attempt to expand his empire. But the purchase turned out to be a costly mistake. Sutter had very little money to begin with and operated almost entirely on credit. The Fort Ross purchase brought his debts to the critical point, and crop failures in 1843 added to the load. To keep himself going, he mortgaged his property, faulted on payments to the Russians, forged checks, and sold his Indian slaves. He somehow managed to stay solvent, and at the same time acted as California's most gracious host. Immigrants and visiting dignitaries found him to be very generous, and the self-styled land baron developed a reputation as a magnanimous man of means. No one realized that Sutter actually lived a very precarious existence.

After Marshall discovered gold in the tailrace of the partially-completed mill, Sutter naively asked all his men to keep the event a secret so he could get some lumber cut and sold. At the same time, he tried to acquire mineral rights to the Coloma land. But the rights weren't granted, the news of the discovery leaked out, and Sutter lost his big chance. Miners divided the Coloma lands to suit themselves, and Sutter was power-

Fortune took him from wealth to poverty.

less to do anything to stop them. Squatters even carved up New Helvetia.

Stories about Sutter, both as a wealthy do-gooder and a debt-ridden despot, reached Europe, and one of his sons decided to visit New Helvetia to get the facts. Young Augustus Sutter found his father in a scandalous situation, living the high life while the debts mounted higher. In a legal move to thwart Russian attempts to dispossess Sutter, all of New Helvetia was transferred into the son's name.

Young Sutter saved his father from destruction. At the suggestion of Sam Brannan, he founded a new city named Sacramento and used the income from the land sales to pay the debts. The fort was sold to raise more money, and Sutter and son moved their headquarters to a hock farm on the Feather River. Since the finances were now in good shape, young Sutter sent for his mother and sister. But before they could arrive, the father somehow managed to get control of the land and money away from his son. When his family landed in California, they found the aging John in the position of a successful country gentleman with almost unlimited income from land sales. In 1850, Augustus left for Mexico, and with him went all semblance of order in the household. Sutter's extravagances got the better of him again, and within a year he had lost all of his property and business interests except the hock farm. Even that had to be mortgaged to pay for lawyers, taxes, interest on loans, and personal expenses.

Sutter tried to claim payments for some of his lost lands, but the courts ruled that most of the original land grants were invalid. Without any means of support, Sutter retired to his farm to live a despondent life. He and his wife fled East when squatters burned down their ranch house. They settled in Lititz, Pennsylvania, where Sutter died on June 18, 1880.

You can step *inside ruins of two-story Uniontown Hotel and Meyers Dance Hall, north of Coloma.*

"Bayley's Folly" *is label given this impressive house at Pilot Hill, once planned to be a fine hotel.*

lady named Susan who had been foolish enough to reject his proposal of marriage.

The town made quite an affair of the proceedings. There was a brass band from Placerville and the crowd was in a holiday mood. But it was the fact that both the doomed came through in the spirit of the occasion that made it a truly memorable event.

With the noose around his neck, Dr. Crane sang several verses of a song he had composed as his departing message and topped off the performance with, "Here I come, Susan!" as the trap fell.

Mickey Free, not to be outdone, rounded out the show with an improvised jig, and then unwittingly climaxed the day by writhing to his death by strangulation after the noose had slipped and failed to snap his neck. His gravestone is still visible in the Coloma cemetery.

The gold discovery site is preserved as part of the 220-acre Marshall Gold Discovery State Historical Park. About 70 per cent of the small town of Coloma is also within the park which includes old stone buildings, a Chinese store, a blacksmith's shop, old horse-drawn vehicles, and a cabin in which Marshall lived after he discovered gold. Further restorations will be completed as funds become available. Buildings are marked for easy identification, and rangers on duty in the museum can provide a detailed map of the park, showing all points of interest. (A replica of the original gold nugget is on display here; the original belongs to the Smithsonian Institution.)

By far the most imposing structure in Coloma is the reconstruction of Sutter's Mill. It wasn't possible to rebuild the mill on the exact location of the original, since the American River has altered its course substantially. But the rebuilders were able to follow the original construction techniques right down to the hand-hewn beams and mortise-and-tenon joints. In fair weather the sawmill is operated electrically about 2 P.M., Saturday and Sunday. Nearby you can watch ore crushed at a two-stamp mill operated at about the same time.

On the hill behind the old town, an imposing bronze statue of James Marshall points to the site of the gold discovery. You can drive a side road up to the monument or take a 1-mile round-trip hike to this statue by way of the Marshall cabin and the old Catholic cemetery.

There are several picnicking areas in town. Recreational activities are closeby. Fishing in the South Fork of the American River is only mediocre, but there are occasional catches of salmon and trout. At Folsom Lake State Recreation Area, there is boating, water-skiing, camping, hiking, swimming, fishing, and picnicking.

The supposedly haunted Vineyard House, south of the park, is now a restaurant. Its wine cellars were built around 1860.

One of the best views of the Coloma Valley is from the Mt. Murphy Road (unpaved). At one time, there was a cannon on top of the hill that was used to signal the arrival of stagecoaches.

Lotus. Now off the beaten trail, Lotus lives a quiet existence with only a few reminders of the early days. The old schoolhouse, opened in 1869, has enjoyed a rebirth as an art gallery. There is also the crumbling ruins of the brick Lohry General Store and the small Uniontown Pioneer Cemetery up on the hill.

About one-half mile north of Lotus, off State 49, are the ruins of the Uniontown Hotel and Meyers Dance Hall, built in 1855.

Pilot Hill. The only building of interest in this old mining town is the three-story Bayley House, which stands beside State 49. Originally planned as a hotel to take care of the people who were supposed to travel on the railroad that was supposed to pass within half a mile of Pilot Hill, the building became "Bayley's Folly" when the Central Pacific chose another route at the last minute.

Plaque *in Georgetown tells of town's history. The main street is unusually wide because of better city planning, after the first shanty and tent town (Growlersburg) was destroyed by fire.*

Alonzo Bayley finished the house in 1862 and tried to operate it anyway, but he never enjoyed any success. The building was sold several times during the next 50 years and even operated as headquarters of a cattle ranch. Today it stands padlocked and unused as a stately reminder of a dream that collapsed.

The town got its name from the "pilot" fires burned on the highest hill to guide pathfinder John C. Fremont's party from the valley to the Sierra.

Chili Bar. Just north of Placerville you can turn off the Mother Lode Highway onto State Highway 193. This winding road dips down and crosses the American River at Chili Bar. In the early days Chileans worked a rich gold bar in the river until many were killed by a smallpox epidemic. Bodies, at first buried on the bar, were later moved to higher ground. A stone monument and plaque now mark the burial site.

Kelsey. Kelseys Diggings, as it was first known, is all but dead, and there is little remaining to suggest that this was once one of the rowdiest of the gold camps, with six hotels and 24 saloons. There is a marker showing the site of James Marshall's blacksmith shop, and a poorly maintained sign at the site of the Union Hotel where he died in 1885. Kelsey lies north of Placerville on State Highway 193.

Garden Valley. This early mining camp originally was named Johnstown after a sailor who first struck it rich. But when the placers had been worked out, residents turned to truck farming and changed the name appropriately.

During the 1930's, the Black Oak Mine was one of the best gold producers in the West.

Georgetown. One of the first things that strikes visitors to Georgetown is the inordinately wide main street that splits the old town. It is wide indeed — a full 100 feet — and it was designed that way as fire protection after a blaze leveled the original tent city in 1852. Even the side streets are wider than usual — 60 feet — just to keep fire from jumping from block to block.

Georgetown got its start in 1849 when George Phipps and a party of sailors worked the stream below the present townsite and struck it rich. The camp was first named Growlersburg, because the nuggets growled in the miners' pans. Tents became the most popular form of architecture, and the streets were lined with miners' shacks and canvas meeting halls. But in 1852 a photographer trying

HISTORIC MOTHER LODE WINERY

Historic D'Agostini Winery, 8 miles east of Plymouth, on the Shenandoah Road, is open to visitors from 9 A.M. to 5 P.M. daily, except major holidays.

In the small tasting room, you can sample the table wines produced from the family vineyards; walk through the original wine cellar — still in use—with its hand-hewn beams, old oak casks, and walls of rock quarried from nearby hills; and even watch the crushing if you stop by in late September or early October.

Now a state historical landmark, the winery was started in 1856 by Adam Uhlinger, a Swiss immigrant, and has been in the D'Agostini family since 1911.

to take a picture of a dead miner in a gambling hall started a fire and the whole town was leveled. It was then that the wide streets were laid out and the town was rebuilt on a more solid scale. By 1855, there were 3,000 people enjoying the cultural life that included events at a town hall and theater.

Georgetown has other notable features. There are a few small stores and a brick I.O.O.F. Hall on the main street that date back to the late 1850's, and some old-fashioned country places and big gardens that were built later in the nineteenth century. At its peak, Georgetown was called the "Pride of the Mountains," and some of the old character is still preserved today.

The Balzar House, a three-story hotel and dance hall named for "Widow Balzar," was built in 1861 and became the town's Opera House in 1870. The Old Armory (1862) originally had only a door, no windows. The Shannon Knox House, oldest building in town, was constructed with lumber shipped around the Horn.

Georgetown even had a good garden nursery that helped build the town into a tree-shaded and flowered family settlement. It is said that the original plants from this nursery gave rise to the spectacular display of wild Scotch broom that covers the hillsides around Georgetown and Greenwood every spring.

Volcanoville. At last count, there were two permanent residents in Volcanoville, a tiny mountain town 9 miles northeast of Georgetown that enjoyed a brief period of glory in the 1850's when

Portrait of an embittered hero.

The saddest figure of the California Gold Rush has to be James Wilson Marshall, the man who started it all. Despite the fact that he was the first to discover gold in Coloma, Marshall never made any money from his discovery, and his fame only led to a life of misery.

Marshall had the fortune — or perhaps the misfortune — to be in the right place at the right time. His gold discovery was an accident, pure and simple, and it is evident that if he had not picked up a few flakes of gold in the tailrace of a mill, then someone else would have found it somewhere else within a year or so. There was just too much gold on the surface to be ignored by the California settlers who were gradually pushing up into the foothills.

James Marshall was born in New Jersey in 1810, was given a moderate education for the day, and was taught his father's trade as a millwright. Like many young men of his time, young James started west after fame and fortune, arriving at Sutter's Fort in July, 1845, about 10 years after leaving New Jersey.

In August, 1847, Sutter and Marshall agreed to build a sawmill in the foothills, with Sutter to provide the men and money and Marshall the leadership. It was when this mill was almost completed that Marshall found gold in the tailrace on January 24, 1848.

During 1848, Marshall and Sutter tried to claim ownership of the Coloma property and charge a commission for any gold found by other miners. Only a few of the most gullible newcomers paid any money to Marshall or honored his self-imposed property rights, and he was forced to sell one-third of his timber and mill rights at the end of the year to raise money. Even though it did him no good, Marshall continued to haggle with the miners and got them so riled up that they finally attacked the mill-hands and drove Marshall off the land.

It was at this point that Marshall seriously undermined his own future. He began to claim supernatural power that enabled him to pinpoint the richest gold deposits. When he refused to divulge the location of any of these rich diggin's, the miners grew very resentful and even threatened to lynch Marshall if he didn't lead them to the treasure.

Marshall fled for his life and tried to start over as just another miner. But his face was too well known, and greedy miners dogged his steps wherever he went in the vain hope that a new bonanza would be uncovered on Marshall's next claim.

This constant harassment turned Marshall into a bitter man. He felt that the world — or at least the state — owed him something for his sensational discovery, and he interpreted every setback as a conscious effort by somebody to cheat him out of his divine rights. He became a recluse, and his eccentric behavior turned away all but a few close friends.

In 1872, the state of California appropriated the discoverer of gold a $200-a-month pension. Marshall moved to Kelsey and built a blacksmith shop. He worked there and lived in the Union Hotel until his death in August, 1885, at the age of 73. The state pension was cut in half after 1874 and eliminated entirely in 1876. During his last years, Marshall was forced to live off handyman jobs, handouts, and the few pennies he could pick up by selling his autograph.

Margaret A. Kelley, a friend of Marshall's during his embittered old age, once wrote that "probably no man ever went to his grave so misunderstood, so misjudged, so misrepresented, so altogether slandered as James W. Marshall." This may be true. But it is also true that Marshall made the worst of his fate, and instead of building on his good fortune, he misplayed it into the instrument of his destruction.

its auriferous gravels were productive. But Volcanoville had no other reason for existence, so the end of the gold meant the end of the town. A fire in 1907 leveled all but a few of its Gold Rush buildings. The only authentic relic of the 1850's is a small bar at the end of the road.

Greenwood. An old trapper, John Greenwood, and his two sons set up store here in 1848 when they found that providing supplies to the hungry miners was more reliable than digging in the cold stream beds. The town grew to respectable proportions in the early years and boasted among other things a well-attended theater. The surrounding countryside is covered with orchards, and Greenwood has managed to carry on as a tiny trading center.

Gold Rush song writer and collector, John A. Stone, known as "Old Putt," lived here and is buried in the tiny cemetery.

Spanish Dry Diggins was located 4 miles north of Greenwood on the Spanish Dry Diggins Road. The first mining was done in 1848 by a party of Spaniards under the leadership of General Andres Pico. Yields of pay dirt were very rich, and the camp was soon surrounded by others along the Middle Fork of the American River. Nothing remains save traces of old mines among the hills.

Cool. Georgetown Road rejoins State 49 at Cool, originally called Cave Valley. Many lime kilns were located in this area, and it was a stage stop on the Auburn-Georgetown Road. When you leave Cool, the present highway descends about 1,000 feet into the American River Canyon. Plans for the Auburn Reservoir, which will deepen and widen the Middle and North Forks of the American River for a distance of some 25 miles, will mean rerouting the Mother Lode Highway as well as other subsidiary roads and bridges.

Greenwood's *Pioneer Cemetery is final resting place for "Old Putt," an early-day Gold Rush song writer. He lies under a stone slab marked "J.A.S." and dated January 24, 1863.*

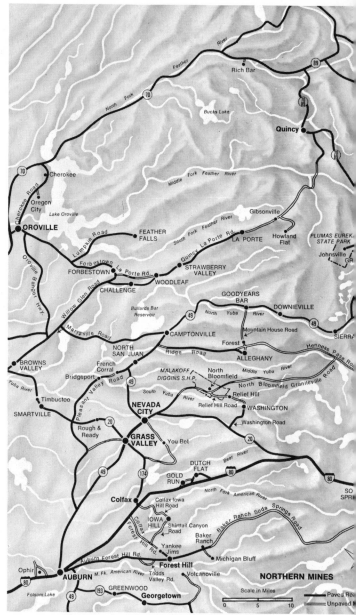

Giant monitors *like the one shown at left and buildings almost hidden by foliage* **(right)** *are more characteristic of the Northern Mines than other sections of the Gold Country. The terrain is more rugged, the weather is cooler, and you may be the only visitor in some towns.*

THE NORTHERN MINES

AUBURN · DUTCH FLAT
GRASS VALLEY · NEVADA CITY
NORTH BLOOMFIELD · OROVILLE

ALTHOUGH THE first prospecting in the Northern Mines was panning for gold along the many mountain streams, deep-quartz mining was first developed here. This is also the birthplace of the highly-destructive hydraulic mining where entire mountain ridges were washed away.

Most of your wanderings off the main highways should be done in summer as side roads are usually unpaved and often impassable because of winter snows and spring run-off. Remember that overnight accommodations are limited to three or four larger cities; it's also wise to check fuel and stock up on supplies in planning a day's outing.

Scenery is spectacular throughout most of the Northern Mines region. It's a land of tall pines, deep gullies, and high mountain ridges. You can picnic beside a waterfall on a backroad to Alleghany or patiently sift sands alongside a rushing river near Downieville, one of the spots recommended for gold panning. And you may be the only tourists in the "almost" ghost towns.

AUBURN AND AROUND

Auburn lies right alongside Interstate 80, but after you turn off into Auburn's picturesque Old Town, you'll immediately overlook much of the modernity in an area now preserved as a National Historic Landmark.

However, it's in the small towns surrounding Auburn where the past is more apparent — Ophir to the west; Foresthill, Yankee Jims, Michigan Bluff, and Iowa Hill to the east; and Colfax, Gold

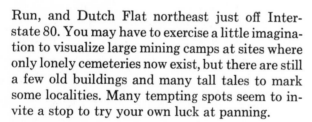

Children investigate *collapsing interior of old, deserted winery located near Auburn's fairgrounds.*

Gold Rush Plaza *buildings in Auburn house antique shops as well as theater used for melodramas.*

Run, and Dutch Flat northeast just off Interstate 80. You may have to exercise a little imagination to visualize large mining camps at sites where only lonely cemeteries now exist, but there are still a few old buildings and many tall tales to mark some localities. Many tempting spots seem to invite a stop to try your own luck at panning.

Auburn. In the spring of 1848 a party of gold seekers, organized by Claude Chana and three fellow Frenchmen, along with 25 Indians, started across the foothills from the Sacramento Valley for Sutter's Mill. The first night out they camped by a stream now known as Auburn Ravine. Chana tried the gravels for gold and in his first pan found three sizable nuggets. This was enough for him. On May 16, 1848, their party pitched tents and started mining operations.

During the summer of that year, the gravels at North Fork Dry Diggings, as the camp was first named, yielded great wealth to those who took

the effort to cart the pay dirt to the stream below. It was commonplace for a miner to wash out $1,000 to $1,500 a day. One account tells of four or five cartloads producing $16,000 in a single day. By 1850, 1,500 miners were busy digging in Auburn Ravine.

Later, a soldier named John S. Woods camped in a spot on the present west Auburn city limit line, giving this particular area the name of Woods' Dry Diggins.

The name, Auburn, first appeared in November of 1849 and probably came from a large group of miners who had come across country with a Volunteer Regiment from Auburn, New York. This busy little settlement became a county seat in 1850, probably because the town's population exceeded that of the rest of what was then Sutter County. The following year Placer County was formed with Auburn remaining the county seat.

After the surface placers were exhausted, quartz

FRATERNAL LODGES—THE NEED FOR COMPANIONSHIP

One of the things that impresses visitors to the Gold Country is the high number of lodge hall buildings that are still standing. An I.O.O.F. or Masonic hall frequently is the most conspicuous ruin in a small town that has been ravaged by fire, and both lodge buildings are almost always included in the best-preserved mining communities. These buildings not only attest to the sound building practices of the lodge founders, but they are also important reflections of an important Gold Rush phenomenon — the need for companionship.

The strongest of the fraternal organizations in the eastern United States — particularly the Odd Fellows and the Masons — sanctioned California lodges early in 1849 to help any of the brethren who might get in trouble far from home. These lodges were badly needed, since many of the men who went broke, got sick, or died were without friends or any source of financial aid.

The fraternities quickly spread through the gold fields, and new lodges opened with each new strike. Organizers had very little trouble recruiting new members, since the lonely miners leaped at every chance to establish some comradeship to help overcome the lonely life in the mines. Those who struck it rich gave freely to building programs, with the result that the lodge halls were made of stone and brick while many other buildings were wood and canvas. Meetings were well-attended, and the local lodge was often the charitable backbone of the community.

When the gold gave out, so did the lodge charters. Hundreds or thousands of members would vanish overnight, many to reappear again on the rolls of some new lodge in some new gold-booming town.

There was one fraternity that didn't quite fit this mold. E Clampus Vitus was founded in 1850 by J. H. Zumwalt of Mokelumne Hill, a man of good humor who decided that the solemn and mysterious fraternal organizations could do with a bit of needling. E Clampus Vitus was a fraternity for non-joiners. It existed only for the purpose of taking in new members, all of whom were held in an office of equal indignity and were ruled by a Noble Grand Humbug. Members were pledged to a life of jollity and informality, and developed such a comradely spirit that a man would have a hard time doing business in many communities if he were not a member.

Despite all the partying and joking, the Clampers managed to do some good work helping the needy. The charity was always anonymous, but the many letters of thanks printed in the newspapers of the day attest to the regard in which the pranksters were held.

E Clampus Vitus was revived in the 1930's, and several historical markers erected by modern Clampers can be spotted in the Gold Country. A wall of the Thompson building in Murphys commemorates some of the early Clampers.

---

mining kept the town booming. However, it wasn't gold that built the modern city you find today. From the very earliest days, Auburn's location has made it a natural transportation center. Both a major transcontinental highway (Interstate 80) and the Southern Pacific Railroad pass through Auburn.

The modern section of Auburn is built on top of a hill. Because the business district migrated up the hill over the years, the early buildings lying below have been left relatively uncovered and untrammeled by modern commerce. The Old Town, with its collection of Gold Rush buildings, is now preserved as a National Historic Landmark.

You can get a complimentary "Guide to Auburn's Old Town" from the Chamber of Commerce at 1101 High Street. Many of the noteworthy buildings are found along Lincoln Way, Court Street, and Commercial Street. Look for the square, four-story firehouse, the Wells Fargo Office that is now a gift shop, the post office that opened in 1849, and a whole block full of attractively decorated offices and shops.

The Placer County Courthouse is not really a Gold Rush building, having been finished in the 1890's, but it is located on the public square that served as the first public hanging yard and graveyard for the town. Nearby is the Pioneer Methodist Church built in 1858.

The Placer County Museum, at the fairgrounds, has several interesting exhibits including replicas of rooms from homes built and used during the early mining days, and displays of Chinese and Indian objects from the same era.

Ophir. The richest diggings around Auburn were in the ravine west of town. Several camps grew up here during the 1850's including Frytown, Virginiatown, Gold Hill, and Spanish Corral. The only one that is still recognizable is Spanish Corral, which was renamed as Ophir when it reigned

THE BELL OF ST. JOSEPH'S

In 1860, Forest Hill, heavily populated by hundreds of Irishmen laying track for the Central Pacific Railroad, had a small church but no resident priest. Young James Cullin, graduate of All Hallows College in Dublin, Ireland, learned of the need of a priest and volunteered for the job, arriving in 1863. Twenty-five years old, tireless and dedicated, he held services in towns all about the area.

One of Father Cullin's Irishmen heard of a bell in San Francisco, brought there by traders who hoped to sell it. It had been cast for a Greek Orthodox Church in Boston, but, by the time it arrived, the church was unable to buy it — so off it journeyed around Cape Horn. Miners and railroaders and other interested Catholics and Protestants bought the bell in the name of Father Cullin for $3,500.

Soon the bell was on its way to Forest Hill — it took six horses, about a hundred men, and a struggle all the way.

St. Joseph's Catholic Church wasn't strong enough to support a 4-ton bell, so a tower was built next to the church. The bell was installed on a Sunday with great ceremony, and then it was rung, taking two men to do the job. The great bell of Forest Hill could be heard 20 miles around.

The old church burned in 1952, but the bell still stands atop a monument.

Forest Hill *retains some of its original old wooden sidewalk. This section is beside a former general store.*

as the largest town in Placer County and an important quartz-mining center. Now, it is only a quiet crossroad. A marker, erected in 1950, describes the old town. Fires and the erosion of time have destroyed all remnants of the Gold Rush.

Todd's Valley. In 1849, Dr. F. W. Todd established a store on his ranch southwest of Forest Hill. It became a stopping place for miners asking for directions to new locations along the ridges and in the canyons to the north and northeast.

Only a cemetery (one of the oldest in the area) now remains. The reputation of this old graveyard has always been as carefully preserved as its grounds. In the days of the gold craze, two stage robbers were apprehended and summarily hung from a nearby tree. Their bodies rest outside the fenced enclosure, deemed inadmissible within the grounds. Some 60 unmarked graves, believed to be those of early-day miners, receive careful attention each May when volunteers arrive to clean up the premises.

Forest Hill. On the ridge between Shirttail Canyon and the Middle Fork of the American River lies Forest Hill, a prosperous mining and trading center during the early 1850's. Gold was first discovered in 1850, but the boom did not really start until the Jenny Lind mine was opened in 1852. This famous mine alone produced over a million dollars in gold by 1880, and the area around Forest Hill produced in excess of $10 million.

One of the best-preserved hydraulic nozzles in the Gold Country is on display near the firehouse. The small collection of old businesses is fronted by wooden sidewalks with the traditional building overhangs.

The Langstaff General Store, oldest building in Forest Hill, served the community for over a hundred years. It was first opened in 1859 by the Garrison family to provide clothing, hardware, and food supplies to the argonauts and was operated continuously as a store until its closing in 1971. Until World War II, gold was exchanged for groceries; the scales rested on a shelf near the cash register.

Shirttail Canyon got its name when two miners prospecting along a creek walked downstream to avoid an obstruction which blocked their view. Rounding the point, they were surprised to see a solitary prospector standing at the edge of the water clad only in a shirt. When the men met, the intruders asked the miner what the place was called. Glancing down at his bare legs and realizing his ludicrous appearance, the miner heartily

A few miles *south of Grass Valley, State Highway 174 passes over the Bear River and an old log flume.*

Concrete-embedded marker *in Red Dog cemetery tells about Little Willie, who fell into a flume in 1864.*

laughed and answered, "Don't know any name for it yet, but we might as well call it Shirttail as anything else."

Michigan Bluff. Best remembered for the extensive hydraulic mining which tore away at the mountainsides in the area, Michigan Bluff, sitting at the end of Forest Hill Road, consists today of a few frame buildings left from the 1880's when the monitors were muzzled. Between 1853 and 1858, approximately $100,000 in bullion was shipped from the region every month.

Michigan City, which was the original town site half a mile away, had its foundations undermined by furious hydraulicking during those five years, so in 1859 the population moved en masse to a location higher on the brow of Sugar Loaf Hill. They called the new camp Michigan Bluff.

A decrepit cottage is still pointed out as the one-time residence of Leland Stanford who operated a store here from 1853 to 1855. However, this is doubtful as Michigan Bluff (then on its first site) was swept by fire in 1857 which destroyed the entire business section in which Stanford's store and living quarters were probably located.

The Chinese cemetery is one of the town's lingering reminders.

Yankee Jims. This town sprang into being under strange circumstances, but the story is a credible one. Yankee Jim, who was not a Yankee but an Australian, was a low character. Rather than dig and wash the good soil of the American River, he stole horses. And nothing was lower than a horse thief in those days. Horse thieves, if caught, were instantly strung up.

Yankee Jim was an old professional, and if one of his victims hadn't bothered to make a careful investigation, the old boy might have gone on indefinitely. But the victim found his horse, and others, too, in a corral hidden away in a high and remote part of a ridge. Yankee Jim hightailed it out of the country just in time to save his neck, and in a way it was sort of a shame.

Because it wasn't much later that a miner wandered into the old corral to do a bit of prospecting and found the ground was rich in free gold.

A crowded camp mushroomed up and a fortune was taken from the diggings — a fortune that could have been Jim's, if it had occurred to him to try his hand at a little honest labor.

Yankee Jims grew into Placer County's largest mining camp; today, you'll find only a few weathered structures.

Dutch Flat *was never destroyed by a serious fire, so many of its old buildings like the hotel* **(top left)** *and tin-roofed homes* **(bottom left)** *remain. Trading post* **(bottom right)** *has added modern conveniences like gas pump. Town's old black hearse is locked up but visible through windows.*

HEARSE HOUSE
OLD VEHICLE ON DISPLAY WAS USED 1870-1925

Iowa Hill. Gold wasn't discovered here until 1853, but there was enough to keep the area thriving until 1858. More than $20 million was taken from the ridge on which the town sits.

The Wells Fargo vault is the only link with this monied past. Fires have been part of Iowa Hill's history since 1857, when the original town was burned to ashes. The last fire was in 1922.

As with many other Gold Country towns, the pioneer cemetery on Banjo Hill provides the most stirring touch with the past.

Hundreds of tunnels honeycomb the mountains around Iowa Hill, tangible proof of a few of the extremely profitable claims worked here. The Morning Star Mine was once known throughout the country. Residents say some large nuggets are still panned occasionally along the North Fork of the American River.

Colfax. This small town, west of Iowa Hill via the Colfax Iowa Hill Road or north of Auburn via Interstate 80, was named after Schuyler Colfax, vice-president under Ulysses S. Grant. Situated in the center of a once prosperous mining region, Colfax was (the Central Pacific Railroad reached Colfax from Sacramento in September, 1865) and still is an important shipping point for lumber and produce.

State Highway 174, between Colfax and Grass Valley, follows the route of a toll road used in the early 1900's — this later became the first official county road in Nevada County. A narrow, bumpy gravel road, U-Bet Road, off of State 174, takes you to the sites of two former hydraulic mining towns, Red Dog and You Bet. There are a few old frame buildings left in the once-flourishing town of Red Dog as well as a small cemetery.

Gold Run. Rich deposits of gold-bearing gravel along an ancient stream bed enabled Gold Run to boom right up to the court-imposed end of hydraulic mining in 1884. The town was founded by O. W. Hollenbeck in 1854 and was first called Mountain Springs. The real rich times arrived with the hydraulic mining operations in 1859.

Only the little shingled Union church, with its shiny new roof, is a memento of the old days. The church was one of many buildings in the Gold Country financed by miners' contributions.

Roadside rests on each side of Interstate 80 in the Gold Run area have antique mining machinery and artifacts on display.

Dutch Flat. Here is one of the most lovable old towns in the Northern Mines. It has a number of significant old buildings, plus pleasant residential areas that give the town a special character.

A German miner, Joseph Dorenbach, and his countrymen started washing the gravels around Dutch Flat in 1851. From 1854 to 1883, the town was one of the principal placer-mining towns in the state.

Millions of dollars in gold were taken out; one nugget alone was worth more than $5,000. The "diggins" lay over the hill about 100 feet north of town in rugged man-made canyons. Hydraulic-mining operations were at their peak here in the 1870's.

Dutch Flat is one of the few Gold Country towns that has not suffered a serious fire, and this blessing shows up in the concentration of century-old buildings along the main street, including the old hotel, I.O.O.F. and Masonic halls, Methodist church, and Runckel home.

Adjoining the pioneer American cemetery above town are the Chinese burial grounds, almost hidden among tall pines. Most of the bodies were removed and taken back to China. The original Chinatown was about a mile above Dutch Flat.

THE WHEEL THAT POWERED THE MINES

One of the most important inventions to come out of the California Gold Rush was the Pelton wheel, a super-efficient waterwheel employing modern turbine principles to produce useful power. The inventor was Lester Pelton of Camptonville, who patented his wheel in 1878.

One of the biggest by far — and one of the last — of the great Pelton wheels is in Grass Valley at the site of the North Star Mining Company in Boston Ravine. This was the largest Pelton wheel in the world when it was installed in 1896. It is 30 feet in diameter, weighs about 10 tons, and worked for 40 years. You can imagine the strength and fine balance that had to be built into it when you realize that, at normal operating speed of 65 revolutions per minute, the rim was moving at the rate of 70 miles per hour.

The Pelton wheel was instantly recognizable by the large number of relatively small buckets affixed to the rim. Each bucket was a single casting or forging divided by a central ridge into two bowl-like scoops. A jet of water delivered from a high-pressure nozzle aimed dead center at the bucket was split by the dividing ridge and turned within the two bowls into two powerful reverse jets that drove the bucket forward.

Pelton wheels are still being manufactured in Philadelphia. They sometimes turn dynamos to generate electricity, but most mining machinery used late in the last century and early in this one was powered by compressed air. Internal-combustion or steam engines in the mines would have asphyxiated the miners, and water in the shafts and tunnels made the use of electric motors uncertain and hazardous. The big wheel in Boston Ravine steadily cranked the massive connecting rods of two 30-inch and two 18-inch pistons to power the hoists, pumps, triphammers, drills, and forges of the North Star Mine, to which the compressed air was delivered through 800 feet of 6-inch pipe, at a pressure of 90 pounds per square inch.

In 1953, during a brief power shortage, an attempt was made to put the North Star's two Pelton wheels back into action, but the old water pipes would not withstand the pressure required for the nozzle. In 1959, the entire plant was sold for scrap. Salvage of the 30-foot wheel came on the very day the acetylene torches were slated to cut it down when an anonymous donor gave $2,000 for its purchase from the wrecking company. In 1961, the land on which the wheel stands was deeded to the city of Grass Valley. The wheel is now part of the Nevada County Historical Mining Museum.

Until the railroad had pushed its way farther up the mountains to the town of Cisco, Dutch Flat was an important stage stop on both the Donner Pass and Henness Pass routes. At the height of its prosperity, the town supported two hotels and dozens of other businesses.

GRASS VALLEY AND WEST

Grass Valley is a town of memories, many of them carefully preserved in the Nevada County Historical Mining Museum. Even the most sophisticated tourist is impressed by the vast display of mining equipment. Happily, there are also still a number of old mine buildings dotting the pine-covered slopes around town. They are open to the public only once a year, but you can get tempting glimpses into the past by driving through the winding back streets.

West of Grass Valley on State 20 are a few hamlets (Rough and Ready, Smartville, Timbuctoo, Browns Valley) worth the slight detour.

Grass Valley. Although this may be the most important gold-mining town in all of California, Grass Valley has kept pace with the changes of modern life. It was here that gold mining hit its peak as an industry. This was not a legendary ground where grizzled miners found big nuggets, but it was the area where big money and big machinery moved in to take as much gold as efficiently as possible. The most important "ruins" left around Grass Valley are not small brick businesses or quaint Chinese quarters, but headframes and inclined shafts of the big mining complexes that once employed thousands of miners.

When the big mining companies moved in, they attracted the important suppliers and peripheral industries, so Grass Valley possessed a broad economic base that was very rare in the Gold Country. The business of deep-quartz mining was developed here, and the hit-and-miss methods of adventurous prospecting were replaced by industrial techniques that required brains and know-how instead of luck and brawn.

The first big strike, however, came about much as it did in many other gold camps — just by accident. The surface diggings in this area were not rich, so only a few of 1849's frenzied prospectors even bothered to set up camp. One of those who did try his luck on the edges of Boston Ravine was George Knight, and he was destined to change the area's fortune overnight.

The story goes that Knight was out chasing his wandering cow in the moonlight when he stubbed his toe on a rocky outcropping. The stumble knocked loose a piece of rock, and Knight noticed the glitter of shining metal. He forgot about his cow, took the piece of rock home and crushed it. A few minutes' work with the gold pan revealed that the rock was gold-bearing quartz, not the first discovered in the Gold Country but by far the most important.

The news of Knight's discovery brought miners in droves, and by summer, the Gold Hill Company had built a mill near the point where the toe-stubbing took place. Between 1850 and 1857 this mine produced $4 million. Other companies followed and within a mile or two of town could be found the Empire, North Star, Pennsylvania, Idaho-Maryland, Brunswick, and others. Hundreds of miles of tunnels and shafts were dug beneath Grass Valley and its neighbor to the north,

Nevada City, and mining continued well into the 1950's. You can get the feel of these busy mining days by visiting the sites of the old mines (see page 97). Just the very size of the surface buildings gives a good idea of the scope of this town's mining boom.

A huge fire in 1855 — probably the most disastrous of the many that ravaged Gold Rush camps — destroyed the 300-odd frame buildings that made up the original community of Grass Valley. It is said that this fire inspired the development of the characteristic heavy masonry walls and iron shutters which now typify a large part of Mother Lode architecture.

In spite of its modern gloss, Grass Valley still exudes an aura of early mining days. The narrow, winding streets and some interesting structures still remain. The most famous residential building left in town is identified with Lola Montez (see page 119) and is at the corner of Mill and Walsh

Best mining museum *in Gold Country is located in Grass Valley's Boston Ravine (lower Mill Street). Here you can see the famed Pelton wheel* (**above**), *which powered mines, and tunnels* (**bottom right**) *used for water release. Grounds of the Bourne Mansion* (**top right**) *are seen on annual mine tour.*

streets. Other buildings of historical note include the Glasson home at 515 Main Street, the Matteson home at 318 Neal Street, the Tremoreaux home at 403 Neal Street, the Watt home at 506 Linden Avenue, and the Bourne Mansion at the Empire Mine.

A visit to the Nevada County Historical Mining Museum in Boston Ravine (Lower Mill Street) is a "must." Formerly the Power Station for the North Star Mine, it is the home of the largest Pelton wheel in the world (see page 94). The museum is open daily from 11 A.M. to 5 P.M. during the summer (50 cents admission for adults, children free with parents). Inside the powerhouse is a large collection of mining artifacts — from pick and shovel to hydraulic nozzle. The 20-stamp mill was recently erected on the grounds and is scheduled to begin operation in 1972.

Rough and Ready. A quiet little village that belies its name, Rough and Ready was founded by a band of Mexican War veterans who took the name from their ex-commander, General Zachary Taylor — "Old Rough and Ready."

Rough and Ready's greatest fame comes from its secession from the Union in 1850 in protest over a miners' tax. The town actually returned to the United States after only a few months, but the rebellion was not officially ended until 1948 when peace was officially made with the federal government so a post office could be opened.

One of the town's most famous incidents reflects the temper of the Gold Rush times. It seems that an unlucky miner was being buried with a regular funeral and all the trimmings, when one of the "mourners" suddenly noticed some gold in the freshly-turned earth at the gravesite. Before the preacher could finish the service, claims had been staked around the coffin and the miners had started to work.

During the 1850's there were more than 300 frame buildings in this town. Today three of Rough and Ready's oldest landmarks are the schoolhouse, the I.O.O.F. Hall, and the blacksmith

Old Toll House *in Rough and Ready is now an antique shop, but it still continues to pull in passers-by.*

Rough and Ready *actually did secede from the Union in 1850 but returned in time to celebrate July 4th.*

A MODERN DAY IN THE MINES

In 1967, the Grass Valley-Nevada City Kiwanis Club inaugurated an Annual Tour of the Mines, which gives visitors an unequaled opportunity to learn about the techniques of quartz mining and to take a look at some of the most important mines in the Grass Valley area.

In fact, this tour may be the only chance you have to see some famous old mines. Some are closed to the public except for this one day; others are difficult to find. And even if you can find the mines on your own, you're likely to be baffled by the function of the strange machinery that is lying around. The Kiwanis tour, held in October, provides guides that tell you what the ruins are ruins of, and just what it was like back in the days when the stamp mills pounded thunderously and the Pelton wheels spun 24 hours a day.

Bus transportation is provided for visitors on the Annual Tour of the Mines. Starting early in the morning and ending sometime in the afternoon, you visit at least three mines, the Nevada County Historical Mining Museum (home of the big Pelton wheel, see page 94), and points of interest in Nevada City including Ott's Assay Office. The tour fee ($5) includes lunch; reservations for the tour are almost a must.

Even though none of the mines is operating on a commercial basis, one of the old vertical stamps has been reactivated at the mining museum for demonstration purposes, and some of the underground passages are opened up so visitors can see how the powerhouse operated.

Among the mines visited are the Empire, New Brunswick, and Idaho-Maryland. The Empire is the biggest and best, and the photogenic ruins extend over many acres. It was also the richest in the Grass Valley area and continued production until 1956. Because the mine has not been completely torn down, you can get a more accurate picture of the complex of buildings and the relative positions of the shaft, mill, and other important points. You also visit the gardens of the beautiful Bourne Mansion next door.

The New Brunswick mine has a picturesque setting but little remains to show how it operated. Ruins of massive concrete ore bins are still standing. The completely vertical shaft was sunk to 900 feet in 1915 to intersect with the incline shaft of the original Brunswick, one of the earliest workings in the district. Boxes by the driveway are cases still containing thousands of exploratory drill samples. The New Brunswick was one of the last of the mines to operate at a profit. It closed down in 1957.

Most mines are dismantled when they are closed, and most of the salvageable material is taken away. This is certainly true at the Idaho-Maryland mine. In the early 1900's, this mine operated on a "share" basis — miners provided their own tools, and owners provided the rest of the necessary machinery. Profits were split equally; unfortunately, this was stopped in the 1920's before a rich vein of ore was struck around the 2,000-foot level. Even during the war years of the 1950's, the mine was averaging $2 million per year. Only a concrete headframe and some shop buildings remain.

Machinery has gradually been moved from the various mines to the mining museum in Boston Ravine. Open weekends in May and from 11 A.M. to 5 P.M. June through the Mine Tour visit, this interesting museum has a wide collection of artifacts, many from no longer existing mines.

Tour information can be obtained from the Grass Valley-Nevada City Kiwanis Club, P. O. Box 2031, Grass Valley, California 95945.

Girls examine drill samples. *Guide gives tour of Empire Mine.* *Stamp mill model fascinates boy.*

shop. The Old Toll House, which charged from 25 cents to $3.00 to pass through, depending on your load, now extracts revenues from motorists by the sale of antiques.

North of State 20, you'll find a fallen tree that was labeled "Slave Girl Tree" when it stood by the side of the road. According to local legend, the tree sprouted from a switch stuck in the ground by slave girl Caroline Allen while she was waiting to have her horse shod at Fippin's Smithy. It was here, at Fippin's, that Lotta Crabtree made her first public appearance (see page 119). Fippin's has recently been painted and is gradually being restored.

Smartville. Originally named Smartsville for James Smart, who built a hotel here in 1856, the post office has been listed since 1867 as Smartville.

Hydraulic mining began around Smartville in the 1860's, and the town thrived until 1883. At one time there were 1,500 miners, 16 saloons, a theater, dance halls, and general stores.

The stately white Church of the Immaculate Conception, which overlooks the main road, rests on stone foundations of the original church built in 1861.

Just south of Smartville on the Hammonton Smartville Road, the Empire Ranch Station, one of the last remaining stations used by the California Stage Company before the advent of railroads, stood for over a century. Only a pile of debris now marks the spot. Halfway up the hill, hidden among oak trees, is a long-neglected graveyard.

Timbuctoo. This once-prospering stage stop, which at the height of hydraulic mining had a population of 1,200, is marked solely by the ruins of a Wells Fargo building. But the old structure has been so badly paint-smeared by vandals that it has lost all character.

Timbuctoo supposedly was named for one of its first miners — a Negro from Africa.

Browns Valley. Named for an early settler who came to this spot in 1850 and took out over $12,000 in gold, it was later the site of many large mines. One of the first stamp mills in California was put up at the Sweet Vengeance Mine by a French company who purchased the mine from Spaniards who had been milling the ore by means of a primitive arrastra.

Almost all that is left of a town that once possessed five hotels, 24 saloons, and numerous stores is an old stone building. Ruins of old mill buildings rise above shafts of once-producing mines.

NEVADA CITY THROUGH SIERRA CITY

Nevada City has acquired a well-deserved reputation for beautiful homes, interesting new shops, and carefully preserved bits of antiquity. It's a good base from which to explore the side roads east of State 49, and it's only a few miles to Malakoff Diggins State Historic Park, site of an impressive example of hydraulic mining.

A turn onto the road to French Corral leads to one of California's last covered bridges. Used by motorists for loop trips between Nevada City and Grass Valley for years, it was finally closed to vehicles in 1971.

From Nevada City, State 49 starts its gradual ascent over Yuba Pass, eventually terminating at the tiny mountain town of Vinton. This area has never attracted large numbers of tourists, and old-timers still recommend places around Downieville for gold panning. Traveling over this terrain should be attempted only during the summer months, because heavy winter snows often close roads.

Nevada City. Some long-time visitors to this part of the country claim that the freeway through Nevada City has done irreparable damage to the old

In and around Nevada City *you can still see much of the area's historical past. Elevated flume* **(bottom left)** *is just outside of town and solitary grave* **(top left)** *is on road to Washington. In May, city has annual home tour* **(top right)** *and antique show that includes crafts display* **(bottom right).**

Finding gold in the California foothills depended a great deal on luck. Getting the gold out of the ground depended on hard, back-breaking work. Gold mining was not an easy task. Most of the miners who eagerly traveled to the gold fields expecting to pick up nuggets off the ground turned away disillusioned when they realized the amount of hard labor required to get a day's wages.

It is true that some of the miners were able to pick up free gold, chisel nuggets out of crevices with a pocket knife, and get thousands of dollars worth of dust in a single pan. But these joys belonged only to a few who were lucky enough to be the first to strike some very rich diggings. Their followers, rarely able to share this quick wealth, were forced to work harder for less money and dream of the day when they would be the first to discover a new bonanza.

Mining evolved from a one-man operation into a big business. The stereotype of the California miner was a solitary figure, kneeling at the edge of a stream and panning carefully while birds sang overhead and his burro browsed contentedly. But this miner represented only the beginning, and he wasn't able to survive long in the intense competition that developed.

Gold mined in the Sierra Nevada foothills came from lode and placer deposits. Lode (hard-rock) deposits contain native gold, mostly in quartz veins, that ascended in mineralized solutions from deep within the earth. Placer deposits contain gold originally in lode deposits which, through erosion and weathering, have been moved to other locations. Water has always been the principal moving force in forming placer deposits.

Panning for gold. Panning was the simplest way to separate placer gold from dirt and rocks. The basic procedure was to shovel some gold-bearing gravels into a shallow pan, add some water, and then carefully swirl the mixture around so the water and light material spilled over the side and the heavy stuff — including gold — settled to the bottom of the pan (see page 108).

Gold panning techniques are centuries-old, and they were put to use in the southern United States several decades before the California Gold Rush. The Mexicans had developed the skills in their own country, using a flat dish called a batea.

The trouble with panning was its slowness. About 20 minutes was needed to wash a single pan and pick up the fine particles of gold. On a good day, one miner could only wash about 50 pans.

Rocking the cradle. A rocker was simply a rectangular wooden box, set on a slope, and mounted on rockers. At the top was a sieve, and at the bottom was a series of cleats or riffles. The dirt was poured into the top, followed by a bucket of water. The cradle was rocked to agitate the mixture and send it flowing through the box. The big rocks were caught in the sieve, the waste ran out the lower end with the water, and the heavy gold fell to the bottom of the box and was caught on the cleats.

The rocker had many advantages. It could be made quickly and moved from site to site. Since water was added by the bucketful, no continuous source was needed, and the rocker became popular at the "dry diggins" where water had to be carried by hand. But the main advantage was that one miner could wash a lot more dirt with a cradle than he could with a pan, and two men working together could wash a cubic yard a day.

The rocker and the gold pan worked reasonably well for coarse gold but were inefficient at trapping the fine particles or "flour" gold. To increase their take from each load, miners began adding small amounts of mercury to the bottom of the cradle. Mercury has the unique ability to trap fine gold while refusing almost everything else. Periodically, the miners would remove the mercury and heat it; the mercury would vaporize, leaving behind the free gold.

The Long Tom was an enlarged, modified cradle. It consisted of a 10 to 20-foot trough, about a foot wide, fitted with a sheet of perforated metal. Underneath this sheet was located the riffle box. At least two men shoveled the pay dirt into the top of the Long Tom. The third man in the crew threw out the big rocks as they collected and kept the pay dirt moving along through the box. Once or twice a day, the gold and sand caught on the riffles would be removed and panned.

The Long Tom could handle a lot of dirt, but it needed a continuous source of fast-moving water. This meant that the miners either had to locate right on the bank of a river or dig ditches to bring the water to the site of rich but dry dirt.

Sluicing. Sluice boxes were longer versions of the Long Tom, built on the theory that more gold would precipitate if the length of the riffle boxes was extended. A number of sluice boxes were often fastened together in a long line, and a whole crew of miners was kept busy shoveling dirt and gravel into the troughs.

Ground sluicing was practiced in a number of ways. One was to dig a shallow ditch and divert river water into it to soften the soil. The miners would then dig the loosened material down a sluice box stationed at the bottom of the ditch. The gold was finally removed from the boxes by panning.

Hydraulic mining. Hydraulic mining was the most efficient method of getting gold out of the ground, but it was also the most destructive to the countryside (see page 114). The operating principle was very simple: if water under pressure could be directed against a bank of soft gravels, the bank would disintegrate very rapidly and the dirt would wash downhill into a series of huge sluice boxes that would catch the gold.

Hydraulicking was introduced in California in 1853 by E. E. Matteson, a Nevada City miner. His was a very simple operation, with a small volume of water carried through a canvas hose and spewed forth through a primitive nozzle fabricated out of sheet metal. Enterprising miners quickly saw the possibilities of hydraulicking, and procedures became more sophisticated. Iron pipe and good hoses replaced the canvas, and big nozzles were fabricated under the names of Monitor and Giant.

The key to hydraulicking was a constant source of water. Some of the big nozzles were 9 inches in diameter and required 30,000 gallons of water a minute. To get the water to the mining sites, very expensive systems of flumes and ditches had to be dug. It is estimated that by 1859, some 5,000 miles of canals and viaducts stretched across the countryside, particularly in the Northern Mines. Single lines were as much as 15 or 20 miles long. The water line always came into the mining area at a high elevation, so that a natural drop of 100 to 400 feet would generate enough force to build up high pressure at the nozzle.

The power of a hydraulic nozzle is hard to describe. One historian compares it with turning a modern fire hose on a sand pile or a bank of snow. Whole mountain slopes could be devoured in a day, with the gravels rushing down through the sluices and out into piles of waste. It was this waste or "slickins" that led to the downfall of hydraulic mining. It clogged the rivers and was carried down into the farmlands where it caused floods, disrupted agriculture, and even discolored San Francisco Bay. The miners were ordered to quit hydraulicking unless they could dispose of the waste; this was impossible so the method was abandoned.

Despite the high volumes of gravels that could be mined by hydraulicking, the system was not very efficient and a lot of gold got away in the fast-moving water that poured through the sluices. The tailings were rich enough to warrant another mining, and enterprising miners working behind the hydraulickers often did very well.

Dredging. Wherever there was enough water to float them, big dredgers could be used to work deep gold-bearing gravels. Buckets could dig up material as much as 100 feet below the water level and dump it into a floating processing plant. The gravels were screened, jiggled, and washed to separate rock from gold and sand. The heavy material was finally forced into barrels where copper plates covered with mercury trapped the gold. The waste was pumped out the rear of the dredger into huge piles that forever ruined the land for any other purpose.

Dredging was first tried in the 1850's, but it did not become popular — or profitable — until the early 1900's.

Quartz mining. It was with hard-rock operations that gold mining in California became a business rather than an adventure. The first mine in California was opened in 1849 at Mariposa, but this system hit its peak in the Northern Mines, particularly around Grass Valley.

Digging the gold-bearing quartz out of the ground was done by two methods. Tunnels were used when the hillside was steep enough to allow a horizontal entrance to be dug into the mountain. Ore was then loaded into mine cars and taken directly to the mill. The other method utilized either a vertical or incline shaft. The vertical shaft was sunk near the vein and "drifts" were dug to intersect the vein at various levels. The incline shaft was sunk following the vein as it descended into the earth, usually between the angles of 30 to 50 degrees. Drifts were dug as needed to work the vein.

Variations or combinations of these methods were used throughout the gold fields in hard-rock mining and in placer mining where the pay dirt was deep or under lava flows. Miners from England and Wales were instrumental in adapting their old-country mining techniques to California and in teaching inexperienced miners how to find the best veins and then follow them.

Once the ore was brought above ground, it had to be crushed. The first crushing equipment was the Mexican arrastra, a primitive arrangement that pulverized the rock between a stationary stone slab and a moving stone slab that was drawn in a circle by mule or manpower. The best crusher was the vertical stamp mill, adapted from European designs. The hammers of these big stamps were lifted by steam and dropped by gravity in a noisy rotation that pounded the ore into workable dust.

Separating the gold from the pulverized ore was first done by panning, but as this proved very inefficient, the gold-bearing material was passed over amalgamation plates to trap the fine gold with mercury. The amalgam was retorted to remove the mercury, the gold was melted and cast into bars. Later, to increase gold recovery, tailings from the amalgamation process were treated by adding cyanide. Then over 90 per cent of the gold could be recovered.

Neat porch *of charming Nevada City home almost invites passers-by to come on in and "sit a spell."*

Many fine examples *of transitional architecture (see page 117) are found along Nevada City's side streets.*

town. They may be right. Even though very few old buildings were torn down to make way for the freeway, the mood of gracious elegance of the town has been rudely shattered by the mass of concrete.

Away from this streak of modernity, Nevada City still manages to be one of the most charming of all the major Gold Rush towns. Its church spires, reaching high above the pine trees and roof tops on the slopes of Deer Creek Ravine, are noticeable as you first enter town. If you drive the side streets, you'll find some old commercial buildings and Victorian houses. The early-day architecture is eye-catching and memory-provoking: broad balconies and roof turrets, mullioned windows and widows' walks, garden gazebos and picket fences. If you want to explore on foot, you can pick up a "walking tour" brochure from the Nevada City Chamber of Commerce at the City Hall.

One of the earliest towns in the Northern Mines, Nevada City sprang up when miners started working the placers along Deer Creek in 1849. It was known by various names — Caldwell's Upper Store, Deer Creek Dry Diggin's, Coyoteville, and finally Nevada. The "City" was added later to distinguish it from the nearby territory that took the same name.

Like other Gold Rush towns, Nevada City start-

ed as a camp, then became a tent village, and then a tinder-box town of wooden buildings. Razed by fire, it was rebuilt, burned, was rebuilt again, and burned again in 1856. It was this last conflagration that caused the citizens to form fire companies and build three good firehouses. Two are still in use by the Nevada City fire department, and the third houses the historical museum. Nearby is Ott's Assay Office, which barely escaped the freeway's path. It was James J. Ott who assayed the ore samples that led to the Comstock silver rush.

Broad Street is the main thoroughfare of town, and along it you'll find the venerable National Hotel (see pages 58-59), the New York Hotel, Methodist church (1864), and red brick Firehouse No. 2. Farther out, on West Broad Street, is the pioneer cemetery.

The old Chinese section was located on Commercial Street, and you'll still find a few of the buildings built in the 1860's. Coyote Street is named after the "coyote holes," small shafts used to get at the gold deposits buried deep in the gravels of old river beds. The Miners' Foundry on Spring Street built the Gold Country's first Pelton wheel. On Prospect Hill stands the Red Castle, a gingerbread-trimmed house, now a small inn (see pages 58-59).

THE LETTERS OF DAME SHIRLEY

The '49ers and their followers were pretty good at letter-writing. Often separated from family and friends, the miners relieved their homesickness and frustrations with long letters to folks back home. Any good-sized public library contains at least a few collections of these letters, preserved as eye-witness accounts of early California. Unfortunately, many of these letters are not very perceptive, and dwell on inconsequential gossip and uninspired comments about climate and the loneliness of life in the mines.

The exception to this pattern are the letters written from Rich Bar by one of the few women of breeding and taste who came to California during the first few years of the Gold Rush. She was Mrs. Louise Amelia Knapp Smith Clappe, "Dame Shirley" to her friends. Dame Shirley spent only one year (1851-1852) in the mines, but that was enough time for her to write a couple of dozen letters back to her sister in "the states." These letters, published many times and available in book form (*The Shirley Letters*, hardcover edition, Alfred A. Knopf; paperback edition, Peregrine Press) are the best first-hand accounts of life in this turbulent period.

Shirley was married to Dr. Fayette Clappe, who came to California from the East for his health and decided to settle in the mining town of Rich Bar rather than San Francisco because of reports he had heard about the bracing mountain air and invigorating climate. Dr. Clappe lasted only a year at Rich Bar, and his career there was undistinguished except for the letter-writing of his observant wife, who was able to put her thoughts down on paper with great wit and style.

Dr. and Mrs. Clappe returned to San Francisco and eventually were divorced. When her health failed, Dame Shirley returned to the East and died in 1906 at the age of 87. Fortunately for modern readers, the letters of Dame Shirley live on, painting a vivid picture of a time and place that is very hard to keep in focus.

Nevada City is now preserving and restoring. The nineteenth-century Nevada Theatre is emerging from under its façade as a movie theater; gaslight fixtures are being installed along Broad Street; and other historic structures such as the Searls building, which housed the law offices of three generations of the Searls family, will soon undergo restoration. This is quite a change from the days when the miners were so eager for wealth they kept the city's streets torn up. A story is told of an angry merchant demanding that a miner stop digging up the street. The miner refused, stating there was no law to prevent him from such action. "Then I'll make a law," replied the indignant merchant and produced his revolver. Destruction of the streets is said to have halted.

One of the most colorful characters in early Nevada City history (or, for that matter, all Gold Country history) was Madame Eleanor Dumont, the lady gambler. She arrived in Nevada City one day in 1854 — young, well-dressed, and of polite demeanor. But it wasn't long before the town learned of her purpose. She opened a vingt-et-un parlor that became the talk of the mines. Charming, proper in every way except that she was a professional gambler, Madame Dumont was a truly unique figure.

For two years she dealt the game, known also as "twenty-one" or "blackjack," to willing Nevada City miners, but as the surface deposits began to peter out, business slowed, and in 1856 Eleanor Dumont, who was to be remembered by all as Madame Moustache, moved on. The name, which followed her in later years as she traveled from camp to camp, was prompted by the dark, downy line on her upper lip, and it summed up the lack of respect that grew as the years tarnished the once-bright young woman.

No one is quite sure where Madame Moustache went. Tradition has it that she traveled all over the West from one boom town to the next, always gambling, always dealing the same game. Twenty-five years after she first stepped off the stage in Nevada City she was found dead near Bodie, a suicide.

French Corral. This little town was named for a Frenchman who built a corral for his mules in 1849. It enjoyed brief prosperity as a center for placer mining.

The Milton Mining and Water Company established the first cross-country phone in the state in 1877 to link its headquarters in French Corral with French Lake, 58 miles away. The brick Wells

Shingles *have fallen away from the covered Bridgeport Bridge, located just south of French Corral. Once used to haul ore to the Sacramento Valley, the single-span bridge is now closed to vehicular traffic.*

Fargo building and the community center — originally built as a hotel and later used as a schoolhouse — both date back to the 1850's.

Two miles southwest of French Corral, across the South Fork of the Yuba River, stands the Bridgeport Bridge, longest (230 feet) remaining single-span covered bridge in the West.

Lumbermill owner David I. Wood built the wooden bridge in 1862 after floods washed out all crossings on the South Fork. For its first 39 years, the bridge was a turnpike toll crossing for wagons carrying freight and supplies to the Northern Mines and the Comstock Lode diggings in Nevada. In 1901 it became a public road crossing and was in use until declared unsafe in 1971 and closed to vehicular traffic.

It has been declared a California State Historical Landmark, and money is being raised to reshingle the bridge and strengthen supporting trusses. A new bridge will be built upstream.

North San Juan. Despite its Spanish name, North San Juan was as Yankee a town as any in the Northern Mines. It is believed to have been named San Juan by a veteran of the Mexican War who saw a resemblance to a hill in Mexico on which a prison of that name stood. "North" was tacked on when the town acquired a post office in 1857.

When San Juan Ridge's hydraulic diggings were being worked, the town was a center for thousands, and it is still the trading center for the few hundred who remain in the area.

WHERE DID EVERYBODY COME FROM AND WHERE DID EVERYBODY GO?

In the spring of 1848 — after James Marshall's discovery but before the actual Gold Rush had really started — there were less than 15,000 people in California, not counting the uncountable Indians. A state census in 1852 revealed that the non-Indian population had swelled to almost 225,000. Where did all the people come from?

Historians estimate that about 65 to 75 per cent came from other parts of the United States. Some 100,000 miners came to California from the East via overland routes during the first three years of the Gold Rush, and the rest either braved the long ocean voyage around the Horn, or went through the agonies of combining two ocean voyages, with the often miserable trip across the Isthmus of Panama.

Of the 25 to 35 per cent of the argonauts who came from outside the United States, the most noticeable influx during the first two or three years was from Latin America. Mexicans — particularly those from the state of Sonora — and Chileans were among the first to hear about the discovery of gold in California, and they swarmed northward to share the wealth. An estimated 5,000 Chileans arrived in California during the first six months of 1849, and the number of Mexicans was even higher. The Mexicans did not stay in California during the winter but chose instead to commute back and forth — working in the mines during the dry season and returning to their homes when the rains arrived.

Of the European countries, the British Isles produced the greatest number of argonauts. Potato famine, economic depression, and social upheavals prompted English, Scots, Irish, and Welsh to give up their homes and make the long voyage to California. Many of them brought valuable mining experience to the gold fields.

The second greatest European contributor was Germany, where political revolution and crop losses prompted emigration in search of wealth and a new life. France, too, lost several thousand to the Gold Rush, because of political instability and depression. A few thousand Scandinavians joined the Rush.

The Chinese got a late start but quickly made up for lost time. In 1850, there were still only 600 Chinese in California. By 1852, their numbers had grown to 25,000. The Japanese did not participate in the Gold Rush at all, since emigration was frowned upon at that time.

While exact figures on immigration are hard to determine because of contradictions and duplications in census reports, it is clear that the California Gold Rush was an international event. And this world-wide drawing power was to have a profound effect on the future population distribution throughout the state.

At the peak of the Gold Rush, some 120,000 miners were busy digging for gold in the California foothills. By 1873, the total was down to 30,000 — and more than half of them were persistent Chinese who laboriously reworked the gravels that weren't worth anyone else's efforts. Where did everybody go?

There is no way of arriving at any exact counts since the miners drifted away over a long period, and not many left their forwarding addresses. But without trying to grasp at figures, it is not difficult to list their probable destinations.

First of all, a lot of the miners went home. Some were disillusioned either by wild stories of streets paved with gold or by their own daydreams, and the hard realities of mining were a great disappointment. Others went back home because of persecution. This is particularly true of the Latin Americans, Frenchmen, and Chinese. Hard-nosed Yankees who ran the "furriners" out of the best diggings and even out of some towns were bad enough. But the cruelest blow was the vindictive Foreign Miners Tax adopted in 1850. All miners who were not citizens had to pay $20 a month for the privilege of mining, and their permits had to be renewed monthly.

Another group of Gold Rush miners was virtually without home or nationality. They followed wherever fortune beckoned and left California in search of new El Dorados—in Nevada, Montana, Australia, British Columbia, or anywhere else that promised overnight fortunes. Nothing could have held this bunch in one place except a supply of rumors and misty promises.

Fortunately for California, a good many of the argonauts decided to stay in the state, even after their dreams of instant wealth had been shattered. There was plenty to do, and no lack of variety in occupations. Some of the miners stayed right in the gold fields and went to work for the big commercial quartz and hydraulic operations that thrived for another thirty years. Others found employment in peripheral industries that supplied the mines — mills, iron foundries, and machine shops.

Those who had adopted mining just because of its get-rich-quick aspects returned to their old professions. After 1860, California began to evolve from a mining state to one based on agriculture, stock raising, lumbering, and commerce. Former farmers and dairymen easily found work in the California valleys and settled down there. Office workers moved into the cities—San Francisco, Sacramento, and Stockton.

Not many of the argonauts really got rich from the Gold Rush. But many of them found a new life in California and stayed around to make notable contributions to the rapid economic growth of the state.

There are several ancient buildings along the town's main street, most of them fast crumbling into decay.

Washington. A lumber town today, the old settlement is surrounded by miniature mountains of boulders that miners a century ago piled up in their backbreaking search for gold. Two old stone buildings — one with the date 1867 carved into its keystone — once served as saloons.

Numerous mining camps were located up and down the banks of the South Fork of the Yuba River. Only names like Keno Bar, Jackass Flat, Lizard Flat, and Brass Wire Bar (worked entirely by Chinese miners in 1880) remain.

Relief Hill. It is believed that the second relief party sent out to aid the Donner party met the refugees and their rescuers near Relief Hill. Long abandoned, there are now only a couple of frame shacks to mark the site of the old town that was first settled in 1853 and had a population of 300 in 1857.

North Bloomfield. Even though North Bloomfield is still inhabited and is in some ways one of the pleasantest communities in the Gold Country, there is a kind of lonely, other-world feeling that many visitors sense when they arrive. Perhaps it is the silence and complete lack of commercial activity. Or perhaps it is the proximity to the Malakoff Diggins (see page 114).

The town was once called "Humbug," in honor of an imaginative, hard-drinking miner who lured dozens of miners to the area with his wild stories about gold-bearing gravels.

Now preserved as part of the Malakoff Diggins State Historic Park, some of the town's old buildings are being restored. Latest addition to the town is St. Columncille's Catholic Church, moved here in 1971 from Birchville (near French Corral). Built in 1860 as training headquarters for the Bridgeport Union Guard, it was taken over for religious use in 1869.

In 1971, one of the old hydraulic monitors was tested for use in the North Bloomfield Homecoming celebration that takes place each June. It lived up to its reputation by washing away a part of the town's only sidewalk.

Camptonville. Named for pioneer blacksmith Robert Campton, this town twice survived the attack of hydraulic monitors by moving each time before its foundations were washed away. Gold was found here in 1852, but real prosperity came only after hydraulic mining started in the late 1860's.

By 1866, Camptonville numbered 1,500 residents. A mile-long plank road, the main street of town, was lined on both sides with more than 30 stores, numerous hotels and boarding houses, and ubiquitous saloons.

You'll find two monuments side by side on the west end of town. One is erected to the memory of Lester Pelton, inventor of the Pelton wheel which was so important in the development of hydroelectric power equipment (see page 94). The other was dedicated by E Clampus Vitus to William "Bull" Meek — who, the marker reads, was "Stage Driver — Wells Fargo Agent — Teamster — Merchant."

Meek is believed to be the only regular stage driver in all the area never to have been robbed by holdup men. Some old-timers will tell you that he escaped being robbed because he regularly carried supplies to a Downieville bordello. According to this theory, the madam and her ladies used their influence on the region's badmen to keep their contact with the rest of the world safe.

Goodyears Bar. This crossing on the Yuba River was named for the brothers Andres and Miles Goodyear, who settled here with a few friends in 1849. The camp boomed in 1852 after word got around that $2,000 was taken from a single wheelbarrow load of dirt. But the good times were short lived, and decline was further hastened by a devastating fire that swept through the town in 1864.

North San Juan (top left), *Washington* (top right), *and North Bloomfield* (bottom left, right) *are within a few miles of Nevada City. Although towns are not too many miles apart, remember a lot of roads in the area don't connect and what looks like a short route may leave you on a river bank.*

One good way to catch some of the spirit of the colorful Gold Rush days is to try your luck with a gold pan. Youngsters especially will find a short session with the gold pan exciting.

Most gold streams were very efficiently gleaned by the early miners, but you may still find gold flakes and small nuggets washed down during spring floods or lost during earlier mining operations. The California Division of Mines and Geology estimates that a prospector willing to toil long hours can still recover 50 cents to $1 a day in gold.

Gold panners' gear. The tools are not hard to come by. Those you don't have around the house you'll find at hardware and general stores in the Gold Country, or at lapidary shops and mining supply firms elsewhere. Basic requirements are: a gold pan, 10 to 18-inch diameter (12-inch is good size for the amateur); pointed shovel for working gravel; prospector's pick; long-handled spoon or butcher knife for digging into crevices; bucket for gravel or concentrate; tweezers for handling tiny grains; hand lens for tweezer-size grains; magnet to remove black sand (magnetic) from concentrate; and small bottle with stopper which can be filled with water to store gold flakes.

Panning: how it's done. Gold panning is a sifting process in which water is used to float off lighter material while heavy gold-bearing particles settle.

Fill the pan full of material taken from nearby bedrock and submerge in water. Pick out the large gravel pieces; wash with fingers until silt is removed.

Raise the pan to just below the surface. Tip it slightly away from you and move in a horizontal circle with a slight jerk each time around, swirling the water to remove the light sand and coarse gravel gently over the lip of the pan. Repeat this "sizing down" several times. Tap the pan now and then in the horizontal position to keep the gold from creeping over the lip of the pan.

Bring the pan out of the water, tilting it away from you. Alternately dip it and rotate it out of the water, letting the water carry away the lighter stones. Brush them out with the back of the hand. Continue this until only the finest sand remains in the pan. Put the concentrate in a bucket to be panned out at the end of the day in the "clean-up pan." At this time, after very carefully removing the excess sand, a magnet can be used to remove the last of the black sand.

For an excellent primer on panning for gold, write the California Division of Mines and Geology, Ferry Building, San Francisco, California 94111, and ask for the free pamphlet titled *Basic Placer Mining*.

Where and when to pan. In the Gold Country, you will find promising streams near roads, resorts, and motels. Many resorts such as Gold Rush, an unusual trailer camp between Coloma and Pilot Hill, offer advice on panning and point out locations of their streams. There's usually a small fee.

Many of the placer streams are on private property, and you must have the owner's permission

Eager panners work creek near Amador City.

Boy checks out possible nugget from black sand.

to pan for gold. However, national forests and other public lands offer some prospecting. The serious prospector will check the ownership map at the county assessor's office; the amateur is usually safe in working where the land is not posted.

Areas with fewer tourists, like back roads in the northern end of the Gold Country, are likely spots. You may find some old hands who will be willing to share their knowledge.

Spring and early summer, when you get the run-off from the mountain snows, is the best time for panning. By fall many streams have dried up.

How to size up a placer. Without going into the geology of placer mining, you can learn a few things a miner looks for before he begins to work the gravels of a particular stream.

Look in old mine tailings. Previous mining activity is one of the best indications of the presence of gold. Commercial mining does not recover all the gold; there is usually some left. Generally, the ground at the tail of an old sluice is a possibility if there is water nearby.

A stream will deposit gold-rich gravels wherever the current slows: where the stream grade decreases, where the river widens, deepens, turns, or joins another stream. Likely places for panning are at the upstream end of gravel bars and the lee side of boulders and obstructions.

Coarse gold tends to be deposited near the point where it enters the stream. A beginner will probably have more luck above the foothills, where the stream grade is at least ½ to 2 feet per 100 feet.

Since gold tends to settle at the very bottom of coarse material, a shallow gravel bar will be easier to work than a deep one. Look for bedrock ledges or riffles in the water or on the immediate banks. Gold often settles in small pockets of gravels in bedrock. Many prospectors use their long-handled spoon or knife to get into crevices. Any soft material is worth panning.

You find gold where other heavy materials collect. This means that streaks of black and colored sands are promising.

Another heavy material that may indicate the presence of gold is "fools' gold," or pyrite. You can distinguish it from gold by the fact that pyrite is often found in cubes, has a brassy luster on freshly-broken surfaces, and will fracture rather than crush as gold will. Mica, too, glitters in a stream and is often mistaken for gold. Mica is light, settles slowly in the water (in contrast to the way gold drops) and scales into flakes. Gold has a yellow color all its own. It has a luster in sun or shade, cuts easily with a knife, and never scales or fractures.

Gold Dust Days. Around the first part of April, gold-panning buffs gather for Amador County's Gold Dust Days. This is a weekend which includes a gem and mineral display at the county fairgrounds in Plymouth, free lessons in "using a pan," in addition to field trips for panning along nearby creeks, and a visit to a small working mine. Write the Amador County Chamber of Commerce, P. O. Box 596, Jackson, California 95642, for additional information.

Spoons and knives make good crevice-digging tools.

"Food" on table is actually a mineral display.

There is very little left today except a few frame buildings and a sparse population.

Forest. This once-lively camp of the 1850's has undergone many name changes. One authority states it was first named Brownsville after a group of sailors (one named Brown) found gold here in 1852, but it was later called Yomana, an Indian name describing the high bluff above town considered to be sacred ground. Another source states it received its present name from a Mrs. Forest Mooney who "dated" her journalistic efforts "Forest City." All agree the last part of the name was dropped in 1895.

Forest is now a quiet little mountain town with only a handful of residents. The town flourished until the 1880's through profitable drift mining. The Live Yankee and Bald Mountain mines were the best known. When quartz mines were developed on the Alleghany side of Pliocene Ridge, most of Forest's population followed the new strikes.

A few of the old buildings are still standing, including a tobacco and confectionery shop. A weathered Catholic church crowns the hill above, and steep-roofed houses cling to the mountains on either side of the canyon.

Alleghany. Built on the bias, Alleghany's houses balance precariously on side hill terraces and look as if they might fall into the ravine at any minute. The streets are narrow and wind down from one level to the next.

At the bottom of the ravine is Kanaka Creek, named after the Hawaiians who made the first big strike in May of 1850. Kanaka Creek was rich in gold and brought a real boom to the primitive mountain country.

The most famous of Alleghany's mines was the Original Sixteen To One (named for one of William Jennings Bryan's presidential campaign slogans). Opened in 1896, it provided the economic backbone of the community until its forced closure in December, 1965. More than $26 million in gold came from this mine, and it is acknowledged by the mining fraternity to be one of the richest, and certainly the most spectacular of California's gold

Many weathered pickets *from this now-neglected fence in Forest have fallen from their frame and rest on ground. You'll find only a few homes and residents left in this tiny mountain town.*

mines, because of its unusually rich high-grade of ore.

The equipment was stripped from this mine in 1967 and only a few boarded-up buildings can be seen today.

You can reach Forest and Alleghany via the Mountain House Road from Goodyears Bar. Driving to Alleghany and on to Forest should not be attempted during the winter as the roads are frequently closed by snow.

Downieville. In one of the highest and most rugged regions of the state, Downieville sits in a natural wooded amphitheater surrounded by lofty, pine-clad mountains.

Fire and flood have done their best to destroy this mountain settlement, but Downieville is still one of the most entrancing gold towns left. The old stone, brick, and frame buildings, many of which were built in the 1860's or earlier, face on quiet, crooked streets that once echoed with the clatter and rumble of freighters and the din that hundreds, sometimes thousands, of miners could raise when they came to town for relaxation and a cup to quench their thirst.

The town was named for Major William Downie who wintered here in 1849. After building cabins in anticipation of a several-month stay, Downie's party began prospecting to occupy their time. They were pleasantly surprised to find the region was rich in gold. By the end of spring "The Forks" (as it was then known) was growing rapidly as news of the rich strikes spread. By June, 1850, about 5,000 people were established here.

The early argonauts really earned their gold— they worked long hours in icy water, had meager supplies, and had trouble finding any lodging. The trail in was almost unpassable for many months, and commodities were scarce and expensive. Shirts sold for $50, boots were $25 to $150 a pair, and potatoes cost $3 a pound. Supplies were improved as the trail grew better, but for a long time saloons that featured many types of elegant fixtures had no mirrors.

Like many other camps along the forks of the Yuba, Downieville has contributed its share of true stories of rich strikes — like that of Tin Cup Diggings where three miners had little trouble filling a cup with dust each day, or of the 60-square-foot claim that gave up over $12,000 in eleven days, or of the 25-pound nugget of solid gold taken 2 miles above the camp.

There are several buildings that are almost as old as the stories. On the main street of town are the present-day Sierra County Museum with walls of schist, the Costa store, and the two-story Craycroft building with its iron doors. On the south side of the Yuba River, the Masonic building, the Native Daughters Hall across the street, the Catholic church and the Methodist church all date from the 1850's and 1860's.

A few blocks east of the museum, the site of Downie's original cabin is marked. Over by the courthouse are the original town gallows, built in 1885 to hang James O'Neal.

Many other buildings which were built in the 1860's cling to the mountainsides above the river. The lovely old residential section adds to the charm which makes Downieville a favorite with tourists.

But it wasn't always quaint and quiet. Downieville has the dubious distinction of being the only camp in the Gold County to have hanged a woman. The story is clouded, and even early newspaper accounts take violently opposing views of the lynching.

Most historians now believe that Juanita, the

In the spring, *waterfalls near Alleghany cascade down hillsides, providing good settings for picnicking.*

fiery Mexican dance hall girl who plunged a knife into the breast of a miner named Jack Cannon, acted in self-defense and was wrongfully lynched. At the time, other miners claimed that the stabbing was unprovoked and that she got what she deserved when they hauled her up on the hastily-built gallows. No one will ever know whether she was actually with child as she claimed before they strung her up, or whether this would have made any difference to the mob. Right or wrong, the news electrified California and made news around the world.

Another story, often told, strikes a humorous vein. It seems that in 1850 a rascal was caught with a pair of stolen boots. The miners quickly gathered to hold court in the business place of the justice of the peace — a saloon. The culprit's guilt was established, but instead of a flogging or worse, he was ordered to buy the house drinks. After several rounds, the guilty one went unnoticed as he quietly slipped out the door taking with him Exhibit A, the boots, and leaving behind the bill for the drinks.

Sierra City. Following the old stage road from Downieville, the Mother Lode Highway sweeps up the canyon of the North Fork of the Yuba River past green alpine meadows and apple orchards. An occasional miner's cabin or farmhouse is seen before you reach Sierra City where the towering Sierra Buttes overshadow the mountain town.

The Sierra Buttes mine, opened by tunnels all the way down to the river, was discovered in 1850 and produced some $17 million in gold. In 1852, the mountains had their revenge when an avalanche of ice and snow crushed every shack and tent in the boom town. It wasn't until 1858 that a permanent settlement was once again established on the townsite. Other catastrophic snow avalanches occurred in 1888 and 1889, killing many people.

Most of the old structures left in town date from the 1870's; the biggest is the Busch building which was built in 1871. Wells Fargo was one of the early tenants.

The three-story, tin roof Zerloff Hotel was built in the 1860's and is still operated by the same

Downieville *of the 1860's* **(above)** *looked remarkably like latter-day photograph* **(left).** *The Yuba River appears a trifle more contained today than shown in the artist's rendering, allowing for the town to expand along both sides of the stream banks.*

family. The hotel's saloon was one of 22 that operated in Sierra City in the old days.

State 49 continues to parallel the North Yuba River, crosses Yuba Pass, and passes through Sattley, Sierraville, and Loyalton before terminating at Vinton.

Johnsville. The best-preserved wood-constructed town in the Northern Mines is Johnsville, in the center of Plumas-Eureka State Park. As a mining camp, Johnsville is a latecomer, having been built in the 1870's by a company of London investors who bought up land in the vicinity.

There are several old buildings in various stages of collapse, and the spot is an excellent one for photographers. Tourists are advised to tread carefully, since most of the buildings are privately owned.

Plumas-Eureka State Park, open year-round, has a good collection of old mining implements and wagons, and the state is working on a long-range program to restore the stamp mill of the Plumas-Eureka Mine and some of the other buildings.

An old boarding house from the mining days has been transformed into the park headquarters and museum. Here, you can see tools and hand-made equipment used for mining.

At the park headquarters is a marker designating this as a pioneer ski area. Winter sports events were held in this region as early as 1860. Today, there is a ski area; however, the park's major activities are hiking, camping, and fishing.

To reach Johnsville, take the Gold Lake Road off State 49 north of Sierra City to Graeagle. From Graeagle, take County Road A14 into Johnsville.

OROVILLE AREA AND EAST

Although Oroville is not on State 49, it has a Gold Rush past. Miners came in 1849, and the area has been the scene of all types of mining from placer to hydraulic. Gold-dredging started here and spread throughout the world.

MALAKOFF'S WOUNDS HAVE SOFTENED WITH TIME

Between 1866 and 1884, the Malakoff Diggins were the scene of the biggest hydraulic-mining operation in the world. Today, they are the biggest mining scar to be found in all the Gold Rush Country. The Diggins themselves have gone through quite a physical change in the century since their mining heyday — an eyesore has become a scenic wonder.

The early miners who first worked the gravels of San Juan Ridge recognized that there was gold in the ground. But the ore was low-grade, and it didn't pay a single miner with a pan or small group with sluice boxes to wash tons of the gravels for only a few grains of gold. It took the large-scale hydraulic-mining companies to bring the ridge into production. By tearing the gravels loose with high-pressure water systems and then washing it in a series of sluice boxes, the hydraulickers could make a profit from gravels that would yield only ten cents a cubic yard.

North Bloomfield mushroomed as soon as the hydraulicking was started, and the town had a population of more than 1,200 in 1880. Hundreds of men were employed getting the gold, and hundreds more worked to build and maintain a 300-mile network of flumes and canals that was needed to bring water to the hydraulic nozzles from special reservoirs in the Sierra.

Hydraulic mining ended in 1884 as a result of an important anti-pollution court decision, but not before it had done terrible things to the land. San Juan Ridge had been re-sculptured by the hand of man. The natural slopes were gone, and in their place were miles of steep cliffs, badly gouged ravines, and acres of waste gravels. Trees and grass were gone, and only the naked rock stood in their place.

But gradually nature softened the heavy-handedness of man. Water and wind rounded the steep slopes into spectacular minarets and pinnacles. Oxidized minerals tinted the gravels with color. Grass and trees grew again, and natural rain-fed lakes formed at the base of the cliffs.

Several thousand acres of San Juan Ridge are now preserved as Malakoff Diggins State Historic Park, with headquarters in North Bloomfield, a town deserted except for the park staff. The park has 30 overnight campsites and two small picnic areas. Activities include swimming at the Blair pond, which once provided the water for hydraulickers, hiking on established trails, or exploring roads and paths that lead nowhere among the debris and standing water below the cliffs.

To reach Malakoff, follow State 49 west and north out of Nevada City for 12 miles to Tyler Road. Take Tyler Road east for 8 miles through North Columbia and follow the signs to Malakoff. At North Columbia you leave pavement and travel over gravel for 7 miles.

Time has softened hydraulic scars on San Juan Ridge.

Old building *with collapsed roof and decaying frame is in Johnsville, center of Plumas-Eureka State Park. Although it makes a picturesque photograph, rangers advise tourists to look from a distance.*

With the completion of the Oroville Dam in 1967, this area has become one of Northern California's major recreational areas. Traces of the not-too-distant past are still found in and around Oroville and on back roads north and east of town.

Oroville. From 1849 through the early 1900's, Oroville was a vigorous mining town. The placers were first worked by hand, then by hydraulic mining until it was outlawed, and finally by dredging operations, which originated in Oroville and spread throughout the world. The ancient river bed on which Oroville is built is so rich in gold that a dredging company once offered to move the whole town just for the right to mine the ground on which it stood.

Thousands of acres of waste tailings left over from the days when dredgers worked the river bottoms were used in the construction of the Oroville Dam, thereby eliminating an eyesore from the landscape and putting the historic old gravels to a useful purpose.

Today, unless you stop and look carefully, you will see little more than a hint of Oroville's gold

boom. Oroville has been turned into one of California's major recreation areas; however, it was at the expense of many interesting mining-day landmarks and natural scenic attractions.

The quiet, tree-shaded town has a dual economic base — the tremendous water projects on the branches of the Feather River, and the thousands of acres of olives, citrus, and deciduous fruit orchards that thrive in the mild climate.

Perhaps the most interesting visit you can make in Oroville is to the Chinese Temple on Broderick Street. This is all that remains of the sizable Chinese community that once flourished in Oroville in the 1870's. Built in 1863, the temple buildings now house extensive displays of tapestries, lamps, gongs, carvings, shrines, sedan chairs, and other magnificent museum pieces. An auxiliary building was erected in 1967 to provide additional space for draperies that were contributed by descendants of the original Chinese colony.

Another valuable stop is the Pioneer and Relics building, where early-day tools and implements are on display. The best-preserved residence in town is the C. F. Lott home on Montgomery

Trim and crisp, *the Judge Lott home in Oroville is a memento of the past—both inside and outside.*

Cherokee. This area was the scene of extensive hydraulic-mining operations, and in the year 1870 alone, produced about $5 million in gold. Some 7,000 people lived in town at that time, and the great hydraulic nozzles ate huge chunks out of the nearby hills; the great scar on Table Mountain is still visible for miles.

The Anti-Debris Act of 1883 ended the hydraulicking and dealt the town a death blow; by 1906, all organized gold mining had ceased, and Cherokee became a ghost town. The ruins of the Spring Valley Assay Office and an old hotel converted into a museum are remaining historical structures.

The first diamonds ever discovered in the United States were picked out of a Cherokee sluice box in 1866. There were many stories about miners finding big gems, and even a far-fetched tale about a fortunate woman who found a two-carat stone in the craw of a Christmas turkey that allegedly had spent its youth in Cherokee. But no company ever made a success out of diamond mining in the region, so most of the stories have to be assigned to the realm of mining legend until some new evidence can be produced.

Rich Bar. The richest gold strike in the Feather River country took place here. Two Germans stumbled across Rich Bar quite by accident in 1850, and after taking $2,900 in their first two pans, they decided to stick around. The lucky partners managed to get more than $30,000 out before the place was overrun with new miners. The gravels turned out to be so rich that each claim was limited to 10 square feet. The total take was something between $14 and $23 million.

Rich Bar enjoyed an exciting life, but it was a brief one. Within six years, the gravels had been worked out, and the miners had disappeared over the hills in search of another dream.

A vivid and colorful picture of life in this old river camp has been preserved by letters written by Mrs. Louise Amelia Knapp Smith Clappe ("Dame Shirley") who lived in Rich Bar from 1851 to 1852 (see page 103).

Nothing of the mining area remains at Rich Bar except decaying headstones in a hillside cemetery and heaps of boulders along the river.

Forbestown. Founded in 1850 by B. F. Forbes, Forbestown was part of the mining scene for about 50 years. The only reminder is the restored Masonic Hall, built in 1857 and now home of the second oldest Masonic lodge in California.

Old Forbestown is now reached by a side road,

Street. The home was built in the 1850's, and today it serves as a museum for period furnishings and displays of photographs.

Just 6½ miles north of Oroville on the Cherokee Road is the Table Mountain area — a natural setting for spring picnicking. Under scattered groves of oak trees, you'll see colorful spring wildflower displays, stretching in all directions. Even the lava mounds sprout with delicate lavender-pink bitterroot (*Lewisia rediviva*).

Oregon City. As early as the fall of 1848, Oregon gold-seekers began arriving in California. Their presence in the mining communities is evidenced by names like Oregon City and Oregon Gulch, on a side road (Oregon Gulch) halfway between Oroville and Cherokee. An old schoolhouse and cemetery still mark Oregon City.

GOLD COUNTRY'S UNIQUE ARCHITECTURE

Early-day Gold Rush buildings tend to have a definite architectural style, although there may be some regional differences. The fundamental appearance of the buildings is due to the use of two specific architectural proportions: the rectangle (twice as long as it is wide, or 2 to 1) and the "golden rectangle," where the length of the rectangle is equal to the diagonal of a square formed by the shorter sides.

You'll find these proportions used in an entire façade, a single story, door or window openings, or panels of the steel shutters. Entrance doors to old offices, stores, banks, and hotels are almost always rectangular. The façades of the courthouse in Mariposa (see page 11) and the Methodist church in Sutter Creek use the 2 to 1 and "golden rectangle" proportions, respectively. The façade and doorways of Volcano's Wells Fargo office, now in ruin, are rectangular, and the Copper Consolidated Mining Company building in Copperopolis is a "golden rectangle" with windows, doors, and steel shutter panels in the 2 to 1 proportion. One of the most beautiful buildings in the Mother Lode—the Prince and Garibardi store in Altaville (see page 49) is a combination of proportions.

The divergent backgrounds of the people who flocked to the gold-rich fields of California between 1849 and 1870 are reflected in the architectural styles of the buildings you see in the Gold Country. Churches were constructed here that would look right at home on a bluff in New England; porches on some homes conjure up images of the old South; details on other buildings recall the Canadian influence.

As you look at the houses and churches of the Gold Rush period, you can see the pioneers brought their past with them. For example, the Methodist church in Sutter Creek, with its cornice and classic low-pitched gable appears to have been moved directly from a New England village green.

The influence of the South is most often seen in the central Gold Country. The hot, sunny climate of the Sierra foothills resembled that of the South, so many buildings were designed with single, double, or multi-storied porches—sometimes on all four sides. These porches were quite narrow, as they served as sun screens rather than as living spaces. The use of iron railings, such as on the Prince and Garibardi store in Altaville, the Yuba Canal building in Nevada City, the old Masonic Hall in Auburn, and the Murphys Hotel in Murphys, also comes directly from the old South.

Wood railings, somewhat like Chinese fretwork in appearance, can be seen on the Imperial Hotel in Amador City, many houses in Columbia, and second-story porches in Amador County. Similar railings may be seen today on the second-story porches of eighteenth-century houses between Montreal and Quebec, Canada.

You'll find few buildings made of adobe in the Gold Country because of the weather and lack of material. The rammed-earth building in Fiddletown and the replica created in Coloma are the only ones of their type. It's important to remember that early-day building was done with readily available materials—local country stone and wood from nearby forests. Except in a few areas, brick was regarded as a status symbol and most brick-front structures have fieldstone sides. A good example of this is the building at Pokerville (see page 72).

Specific architectural features, such as the double porch post, are often seen in the Gold Country. Many of the double porch posts are delicately made, with great variety in the capitals. As the style progressed, builders began to add ornament between each pair of posts so that seldom are two alike. The I.O.O.F. building at Mokelumne Hill (see page 62) is unique in having double porch posts in metal. Even today, new houses in the Gold Country have porch roofs supported by double posts; unfortunately, not all of them have the same high quality of craftsmanship.

There are many local and regional architectural differences within the Gold Country. Some elements may exist only in one county, or they may exist in widely separate areas. One such example is the two-centered arch; there are very few in the old section of Oroville and over in Virginia City, Nevada, but they can be found in great number in Amador County. Many buildings in Calaveras County have asymetrical roofs—where the two slopes of a gabled roof are different. Other regional differences include the jack arch and partial attic story found on brick buildings in Auburn, and the square high hip roofs in Calaveras County. Also, roofs seem to pitch more steeply as you move north, probably due to weather conditions.

Although the Gold Rush was a frontier region and time was of the essence, a great deal of craftsmanship went into a structure. Towns seemed to maintain a continuous style of architecture against tremendous odds. Fire often destroyed the whole town overnight. It is said that a disastrous fire in Grass Valley inspired the iron shutters and heavy masonry walls that now stand throughout the Gold Country. Certainly tin roofs were used as a fire deterrent.

After 1870, the hard-rock businessman-type miner took over, other businesses began to prosper, new people came to town, and architecture took on the contemporary Victorian style, as seen in many homes of Nevada City.

about a mile north of the present post office and stores which perpetuate the name.

Woodleaf. This tiny settlement was founded by Charles Barker in 1850 and was first known as Barker's Ranch. James Wood took over the place in the late 1850's and built the Woodville House, a two-story brick hotel which is still the biggest landmark for miles.

Strawberry Valley. There is some confusion about the origin of this town's name — either it came from wild berries that grew in the area, or it is the combination of names of miners, Straw and Berry.

At any rate, Strawberry Valley was a commercial center for many mines that sprouted into life in the surrounding valleys during the 1850's. At one time, there were dozens of stores and hotels. Now, only the Columbus Hotel (still with its original well) stands by the side of the main road.

La Porte. A well-populated hydraulic-mining center before the Anti-Debris Act was passed, La Porte is now a small mountain town with only the crumbling Wells Fargo office building and the Union Hotel as reminders of the good old days.

The house in which Lotta Crabtree (see page 119) lived for a while as a child was destroyed by fire. A marker at the west end of town marks the site of the Rabbit Creek Hotel and commemorates the discovery of gold on Rabbit Creek in 1850.

Gibsonville and Howland Flat. This rugged section of mountains was settled in 1850. Gibsonville, perched on a windswept ridge overlooking Slate Creek, was named for one of the early prospectors. Only a few bleached houses mark the site.

Howland Flat was one of the most populous camps in the Northern Mines for a short time because of its rich hydraulic diggings. The site of Poker Flat — the setting for one of Bret Harte's most famous stories, "The Outcasts of Poker Flat" — can be reached via a 3-mile trail from Howland Flat.

Other mining camps established around this area at about the same time include Queen City, Port Wine, Poverty Hill, and Scales. Port Wine, named by prospectors who found a cask of wine hidden in a nearby canyon, is still marked by an old stone store building, a cemetery, and large piles of diggings.

Cherokee's history *has legends of diamond mining as well as gold prospecting. Stone walls of assay office* **(above)** *and old building across the street* **(top right)** *are about all that remain of the town today. Deserted schoolhouse* **(bottom right)** *is in Oregon City, between Oroville and Cherokee.*

LOLA AND LOTTA—GLAMOUR IN THE MINING CAMPS

Lola taught.   *Lotta learned.*

There are no more famous names in the history of the Northern Mines than those of Lola Montez and Lotta Crabtree. They injected an element of glamour into the often tawdry routine of the mining camps, and stories about this flashy pair are easy to come by and often repeated.

Lola Montez — born Eliza Gilbert in Ireland in 1818 — was a sensation in Europe during the 1840's, both for her theatrical talents and her personal life. She was the mistress of Ludwig of Bavaria for two years and later presided over soirees where the Continent's foremost literary and artistic figures held sway. Franz Liszt, George Sand, Victor Hugo, and Alexander Dumas were among her intimates.

Lola embarked on a tour of America in 1852 and eventually made it to San Francisco the following year. Her famous beauty and notoriety packed the audiences, but her mediocre dancing talents — even in the exotic Spider Dance — were somewhat disappointing to the jaded San Franciscans. She received an even harsher reception at performances in Sacramento and Marysville, and finally descended on Grass Valley where she decided to forsake the theater and retire. She moved into the house on Mill Street that is still standing today (not open to the public) where she lived with grizzly bears and monkeys for pets, threw big parties, and gave occasional performances for local crowds.

Among the most famous — and least credible

— stories about Lola Montez had her performing her provocative, miniskirted dance at the door of an objecting minister and horsewhipping a newspaper editor for printing some inaccuracy about her.

When not living the high life, Lola stayed around the house and even managed to get a garden started. School children passed her house regularly, and one day, little 7-year-old Lotta Crabtree stopped by for a visit. The Crabtrees lived just down the block from the Montez house, and Lola and Lotta became good friends. The bubbling, irrepressible little girl caught the aging beauty's fancy, and Lola began to teach her little friend some songs and dances. Lotta learned very quickly and was soon performing for Miss Montez's guests. Legend has it that Lola took the little girl with her on a trip to Rough and Ready, and Lotta gave her first public performance on top of the anvil in Fippin's Smithy while the talented blacksmith pounded out accompaniment with his hammer.

In 1854 — about a year after Lola and Lotta first met — the Crabtrees moved to La Porte. Student and teacher were separated, but Lotta was ready to go out on her own. She went on the stage of a local tavern at the age of 8 and was a smash success. The miners showered the stage with coins and nuggets, and Lotta was launched on a busy and very successful career. She toured the mines for years, often in grueling one-night stands, and built a huge following. Finally, she went to San Francisco for successful engagements, and then to New York in 1864 and on to international fame. She retired at an early age and lived gracefully until 1924. At the time of her death, her estate totaled $4 million.

Fate was not so kind to her teacher. Lola Montez grew weary of "retirement" in Grass Valley and went to Australia on tour in 1855. But she failed there and returned to the United States to try her hand at lecturing, which resulted in still another failure. Her health began to give out, and once-wealthy Lola Montez spent a miserable final few years before passing away in New York at the age of 43. The year was 1861, just about the time that Lotta Crabtree was emerging as the darling of San Francisco and starting on her great career.

Lola's Grass Valley house has a spooky quality about it, hidden as it is behind gnarled trees and overgrown bushes. Its air of mystery seems to fit the former owner well. But for all her questionable qualities, it will remain to her eternal credit that Lola Montez took the time, trouble, and energy to start little Lotta Crabtree on one of the most illustrious careers in the history of the stage.

CALENDAR OF EVENTS

Listed below is a sampling of celebrations held throughout the Gold Country. Although many events are held annually on set dates, others depend on such things as weather and funds. We recommend you check with the Chambers of Commerce (names and addresses at bottom of page 121) for definite dates and additional information on these or other events occurring in their area.

	EVENT	LOCATION	COUNTY
January	NASTR Ski Races	Dodge Ridge	Tuolumne
	Snowmobile Races	Leland Meadows	Tuolumne
	Gold Discovery Days	Coloma	El Dorado
February	Flea Market	Sutter Creek	Amador
	Mountain Men Antique Auction	Jackson	Amador
March	Daffodil Hill Bulb Show	Daffodil Hill	Amador
April	Daffodil Hill Bulb Show	Daffodil Hill	Amador
	Square Dancers Festival	Sonora	Tuolumne
	Gold Nugget Celebration	Paradise	Butte
	Gold Dust Days	Plymouth	Amador
	Art Show	Auburn	Placer
May	Fireman's Muster	Columbia State Park	Tuolumne
	Mother Lode Round-up	Sonora	Tuolumne
	Art Show	Amador City	Amador
	Calaveras County Fair and Jumping Frog Contest	Angels Camp	Calaveras
	Fly-in Breakfast	Columbia State Park	Tuolumne
	Homecoming Picnic & Parade	Ione	Amador
	Annual Homes Tour	Auburn	Placer
	Flea Market	Sutter Creek	Amador
	Antique Fair	Nevada City	Nevada
	Annual Spring Historical House Tour	Nevada City	Nevada
	Homecoming and Fiddler's Contest	Fiddletown	Amador
	Coarsegold Annual Rodeo	Coarsegold	Madera
	Melodramas	see pages 42-43	
June	Annual Mother Lode Art Exhibition	Sonora	Tuolumne
	Annual Flea Market	Mariposa	Mariposa
	Malakoff Homecoming	North Bloomfield	Nevada
	Twain Harte Tuolumne Jubilee	Tuolumne	Tuolumne
	Italian Picnic & Parade	Sutter Creek	Amador
	El Dorado County Fair	Placerville	El Dorado
	Kit Carson Days	Jackson	Amador
	Bicycle Races	Nevada City	Nevada
	End of Highway 50 Wagon Train	Placerville	El Dorado

	EVENT	LOCATION	COUNTY
July	West Point Centennial Days	West Point	Calaveras
	Murphys Homecoming	Murphys	Calaveras
	Old Fashioned 4th of July	Columbia State Park, Mokelumne Hill, Nevada City and Grass Valley (alternate years)	
	Pony Express Days	Pollock Pines	El Dorado
	Mother Lode Fair	Sonora	Tuolumne
	"Junk in July"	Auburn	Placer
August	Amador County Fair	Plymouth	Amador
	Nevada County District Fair	Grass Valley	Nevada
	El Dorado Days	Mountain Ranch	Calaveras
	Twain Harte Annual Horse Show	Center Camp	Tuolumne
September	Black Bart Days	San Andreas	Calaveras
	Mariposa County Fair & Homecoming	Mariposa	Mariposa
	Mi-Wok Indian Acorn Festival	Tuolumne Rancheria	Tuolumne
	Constitution Day Parade	Nevada City	Nevada
	Auburn District Fair	Auburn	Placer
	Sierra Mountaineer Days	Oakhurst	Madera
October	Arabian Horse Show	Mariposa	Mariposa
	Mother Lode Quarterhorse Show	Sonora	Tuolumne
	Art Show	Amador City	Amador
	Day in the Mines	Grass Valley	Nevada
	Apple Hill Smorgy	Camino	El Dorado
	Flea Market	Sutter Creek	Amador
	Trade Fair	Nevada City	Nevada
	Columbus Day Parade	Jackson	Amador
	Miwok Festival	Indian Grinding Rock S.H.P.	Amador
November	Crafts Fair	Pioneer	Amador
	Artists Christmas Fair	Nevada City	Nevada
December	Open House	Jackson	Amador
	Christmas Art Exhibitions	many towns	

CHAMBERS OF COMMERCE

Amador County: Amador County Chamber of Commerce, P. O. Box 596, Jackson 95642. **Butte County:** Paradise Chamber of Commerce, P. O. Box 251, Paradise 95969. **Calaveras County:** Calaveras County Chamber of Commerce, P. O. Box 177, San Andreas 95249. **El Dorado County:** El Dorado County Chamber of Commerce, P. O. Box 268, Placerville 95667. Hangtown Chamber of Commerce, P. O. Box 151, Placerville 95667. **Madera County:** (for Oakhurst and Coarsegold) Oakhurst Chamber of Commerce, P. O. Box 374, Oakhurst 93644. **Mariposa County:** Mariposa County Chamber of Commerce, Mariposa 95338. **Nevada County:** Grass Valley Chamber of Commerce, 106 So. Auburn, Grass Valley 95945. Nevada City Chamber of Commerce, City Hall, Nevada City 95959. **Placer County:** Placer County Chamber of Commerce, 321 Commercial St., Auburn 95603. Auburn Area Chamber of Commerce, 1101 High St., Auburn 95603. **Tuolumne County:** Tuolumne County Chamber of Commerce, P. O. Box 277, Sonora 95370.

THE TIME OF THE ARGONAUTS AN HISTORICAL CHRONOLOGY

It is often difficult to keep the complete picture of the California Gold Rush in mind as you travel along State Highway 49. Each town offers but a small bit of history, and the grand scheme of things tends to get lost in a morass of dates, names, and details. The historical chronology here is intended to provide a general reference guide for you as you travel through the Gold Rush Country.

Because of space limitations, some discoveries and events have been omitted, but enough is included to give you a general idea of how the Gold Rush spread through California. Greatest emphasis is placed on the years 1848 to 1851, since this was the primary period of discovery.

Notable political events also are listed to put the Gold Rush in proper perspective with the development of California as a territory and a state. Additional details are readily available in any of the well-written histories of the state (see bibliography, page 125).

1839 August. Swiss-born John Sutter arrives at the confluence of the Sacramento and American rivers to start Northern California's first inland settlement.

1841 November 4. The first California pioneers, organized by John Bidwell, arrive in the San Joaquin Valley after leaving Independence, Missouri, on May 19.

1842 March. While digging onions to eat for lunch, rancher Francisco Lopez finds gold in the San Fernando Hills, about 45 miles north of Los Angeles. Within two months, about 100 miners are working the placers. But the supply is limited and when John Bidwell visits the site in 1845, he finds about 30 miners working hard for 30 cents a day.

1842 August. General Manuel Micheltorena, the last of the Mexican governors, takes office in Monterey.

1845 March. Micheltorena is driven from the state by *Californios,* who fight among themselves for power.

1845 July. James Marshall arrives at Sutter's Fort on a wagon train from Oregon.

1846 March. Supposedly acting on orders from President Polk, Captain John C. Fremont raises the American flag on a peak in the Salinas Valley. The gesture is ineffective.

1846 May 13. War begins between the U.S. and Mexico.

1846 June 14. Believing that the *Californios* are going to run them out of the state, a group of American ranchers ride into Sonoma, capture General Mariano Vallejo, and declare the Bear Flag Republic.

1846 July 7. Commodore John Sloat lands the U. S. Pacific Fleet at Monterey, raises the American flag, and proclaims California part of the United States. Two days later, the U. S. flag replaces the Bear Flag at Sonoma and is raised on Yerba Buena Island.

1846 October. The first storms of what will be an exceptionally heavy winter trap the immigrant wagon train led by George Donner in the Sierra. By spring, 39 of the 87 members of the train will be dead of cold and starvation in the greatest tragedy of the California migration.

1847 January 13. The war in California is ended as Captain Fremont and General Pico, leader of the *Californios,* sign the Cahuenga Capitulation.

1847 Late January. The Mormon Battalion—300 recruits from Utah—arrive to fight in the war with Mexico. They are too late for the fighting, but some decide to stay and work for John Sutter.

1847 February 10. John Fremont becomes the owner of a big tract of land near Mariposa which appears worthless at the time but will ultimately become the richest in the Southern Mines.

1847 May 16. At Sutter's instruction, James Marshall sets out for the foothills to select a site for a sawmill. Marshall selects a valley on the American River that the Indians call *Culluma.*

1847 August 27. Sutter and Marshall sign an agreement to build the mill, with Sutter to provide the manpower (primarily members of the Mormon Battalion) and Marshall the know-how. Work begins in September.

1848 January 24. While examining the tailrace of the partially completed sawmill, Marshall notices something glittering in the rocks. He picks up a small piece of metal and after a few preliminary tests decides that he has found some gold.

1848 January 28. Marshall arrives in Sutter's Fort with his precious metal. Sutter subjects it to several more tests and proves conclusively that Marshall has discovered gold.

1848 February 2. The treaty of Guadalupe Hidalgo is signed ending the Mexican War, and the California territory is formally ceded to the United States.

1848 February 6. Although they are pledged to secrecy about Marshall's discovery, the workers at the mill become the first argonauts by sneaking off to pry gold nuggets out of the rock with penknives.

1848 Mid-February. Sutter sends Charles Bennett on a secret mission to Monterey to secure land rights at Coloma. But Bennett cannot keep the discovery of gold to himself and spreads the word to everyone he meets.

1848 March. Mormon Island becomes the first mining camp outside of Coloma. Sutter reports that he is losing all of his staff to the gold fields.

1848 March 11. The sawmill at Coloma is finished. It will be operated sporadically for about five years before being torn down by miners who need the lumber for new buildings.

1848 March 15. The first story of the gold discovery is printed in a San Francisco newspaper, but not many people pay any attention to the report.

1848 Late March. John Bidwell visits Coloma and decides there must be gold in the northern mountains. He makes a big strike at Bidwell's Bar in April.

1848 April 1. San Francisco sends a special messenger to the East Coast with news of the rumored discovery.

1848 May. By now, 800 miners are working at Coloma, Mormon Island, Kelseys Diggings, and other areas on both sides of Sutter's Mill. One of the richest strikes of all is made at Dry Diggin's, which will ultimately become Placerville, and gold is discovered on the Yuba River near Long Barn. Claude Chana and a group of miners make a strike at North Fork Dry Diggin's—later to become Auburn. George Angel builds a trading post on Calaveritas Creek and Angels Camp is born. Drytown is settled. After early skepticism, San Franciscans are finally convinced that gold really has been found and the rush to the foothills begins.

1848 June 1. The number of miners now working the foothills is estimated at 2,000.

1848 June 14. The last of the San Francisco newspapers suspends operation for lack of readers, and practically all business in the city is suspended.

1848 June 20. A special messenger arrives in Monterey with a pocketful of nuggets dug near Coloma. Residents are finally convinced of Marshall's discovery and make a mass exodus.

1848 June 24. A newspaper in Hawaii reports the discovery, and the first ships loaded with argonauts leave in July.

1848 July. Some 4,000 miners are now working in the foothills. Col. R. B. Mason, Military Governor of California, visits

Coloma and confirms the richness of the diggings. News of the discovery reaches Los Angeles and the first miners start north. John Sutter and a crew of Indians find gold at Sutter Creek, and John and Daniel Murphy start the town that is to carry their name.

1848 August. First rumors reach the East Coast, but there is no official confirmation yet. A Chilean ship reaches Valparaiso with the news, and several thousand men start immediately for California. Ships from Hawaii bring the news to Oregon, and wagon trains start south. New mining camps spring up at Jackson, Woods Crossing, Tuttletown, Fiddletown, and Timbuctoo. Friendly Indians lead James Carson to gold on Carson Creek. Sonorian Camp (Sonora) becomes the southernmost mining camp to be settled in 1848.

1848 September. Heat and sickness in the mines cause some of the weaker men to abandon the diggings and return to the valleys, many settling around Sutter's Fort. Washington, D. C., receives official confirmation of Marshall's discovery.

1848 October. The number of miners has grown to 8,000. Mexico learns of the discovery, and a great migration is prepared for the following spring.

1848 November. Mokelumne Hill is founded. Rain and cold force more miners out of the hills, and only the hardy remain to continue working through the winter. On the East Coast, the first ships loaded with argonauts leave for California and more get ready to sail from New York, Boston, Salem, Norfolk, Philadelphia, and Baltimore.

1848 December 5. President Polk's message to Congress confirms the California gold discovery. His message is backed up by a box filled with gold dust that is put on public display. The fever takes hold. Buffeted by the turn of events, James Marshall and John Sutter sell most of their interests in Coloma.

1848 December 23. A newspaper in Sydney, Australia, publishes news of the discovery; hundreds of miners set sail.

1849 January. Five California trading and mining companies are started in London, and all Europe begins to send ships loaded with miners.

1849 February 28. The steamship *California*—the first of the Pacific Mail steamers—arrives in San Francisco with the first load of '49ers.

1849 Spring. Prospecting starts again. Gold is discovered at Jacksonville, mining begins at Jenny Lind, and Goodyears Bar is settled by Miles Goodyear.

1849 May. The great procession of overland wagon trains begins from St. Joseph and Independence, Missouri. Some 4,000 miners from Sonora, Mexico, are on their way north.

1849 July. The first of the overland wagon trains arrives in the Sacramento Valley. By now, 600 vessels have arrived in San Francisco Bay, and both crews and passengers head immediately for the mines.

1849 September. The first miners work the gravels at Downieville; the town is started in November by Major Downie.

1849 October. The first of the European emigrants begin to arrive. Dr. A. B. Caldwell builds a general store on Deer Creek and Nevada City is born. Chinese Camp is settled, James Savage begins mining at Big Oak Flat, and the first miners set up camp at Coulterville, French Corral, Volcano, San Andreas, Groveland, Shaws Flat, and Oroville.

1849 November 13. A state constitution is ratified, a governor is elected, and senators and assemblymen are named—even though the California territory is not legally a state.

1849 Winter. It is estimated that 42,000 argonauts have arrived by land during the year, and another 39,000 have come by sea from all parts of the world. Heavy rains force many miners out of the hills and into Sacramento and San Francisco. Their presence prompts the cities to realize their inadequacies and promotes improvements such as paved streets, sidewalks, and sewers.

1850 Spring. In the Southern Mines, Mount Bullion is settled, and the first private mint in California opens at Mt. Ophir.

1850 March. Mexicans discover gold a few miles north of Sonora. On March 27 a group of American miners do the same thing, and the rush is started at Columbia.

1850 April. Yankee dislike for foreigners results in the legislative adoption of a Foreign Miners Tax of $20 a month, renewable every month. It is supposedly leveled against all "furriners" but is enforced chiefly against the Spanish-Americans and the Chinese.

1850 June. An accidental discovery of gold-bearing quartz on Gold Hill starts the rush to Grass Valley.

1850 Summer. Kanaka Creek below Alleghany is first mined by Hawaiians. A new settlement grows at Growlersburg (Georgetown), and mining starts in Onion Valley near La Porte. Michigan Bluff and Sierra City have their first success; Washington is founded as Indian Camp.

1850 September 9. California is admitted into the Union as the 31st state.

1850 October 18. The steamer *Oregon* brings the news of statehood to San Francisco.

1850 Winter. During this year, 55,000 people have arrived on the overland caravans, and another 36,000 have come by sea.

1851 February. The first quartz mine in Amador County is discovered at Amador Creek. This, plus the findings at Grass Valley, start a big boom in quartz mining.

1851 March 14. The Foreign Miners Tax is repealed—at least temporarily.

1851 April. Gold is discovered in Australia, and the tide of argonauts across the Pacific is reversed. Virtually all of the main California gold fields are settled by now, and prospectors must move on to find new diggings. When gold is discovered in Oregon's Rogue River country, more miners give up California in search of greener pastures.

1852 May 4. A new license fee of $3 (later to be raised to $4) is assessed against all foreign miners.

1852 Summer. Mining starts at La Grange and Camptonville.

1853 March. E. E. Matteson first forces water under pressure through a nozzle to wash a gravel bank, and hydraulic mining is born.

1853 Summer. Lola Montez settles in Grass Valley; Christian Kientz discovers gold at North San Juan. Michael Savage begins mining at Forest Hill. Iowa Hill becomes a boom town. After a time of depression, confidence is restored in quartz mining that will last for decades.

1854 Spring. Bret Harte arrives in California for a 17-year stay, most of which is spent far from the mines. But his brief experiences with frontiersmen provide enough material for many literary works.

1854 Summer. Lotta Crabtree gives her performance for the miners at La Porte and is launched on a long and successful stage career.

1854 Fall. Gold is discovered on the Kern River, drawing more miners out of Northern California. Still others sail for Peru, but the stories of rich mines there turn out to be only rumors.

1855 January. Snowshoe Thompson makes his first skiing trip across the Sierra in winter to start a unique career as one of the most remarkable postmen in history.

1855 August 11. Tom Bell attempts the first stage robbery for gold, but he is foiled and ultimately captured.

1855 October 25. The great tong war is held at Chinese Camp.

1859 July 1. The *Nevada Journal* in Nevada City publishes the results of assays of ore specimens brought from the state of Nevada, which show that silver as well as gold has been discovered. The great rush to the Comstock begins. Many historians regard this as the official end of the California Gold Rush.

1860 April 13. The first westbound rider of the Pony Express reaches San Francisco after leaving St. Joseph, Missouri, on April 3.

1861 Summer. Mark Twain arrives in the West. He will stay until 1865 and write some of the best of all the Gold Country stories.

1862 Winter. Unprecedented storms produce terrible floods that badly damage river communities and illustrate how unrestricted hydraulic mining chokes the river beds.

1877 Summer. Black Bart stages his first successful holdup.

1880 June 18. John Sutter dies in Pennsylvania.

1884 January 23. The Sawyer Decision following passage of the Anti-Debris Act of 1883 closes all the hydraulic mines in California.

1885 August 10. James Marshall dies at Kelsey.

1893 Summer. The Caminetti Act permits hydraulic mines to reopen if debris dams are built to catch all of the silt before it can clog the rivers. A few attempts are made to meet the requirements, but the cost is too great and hydraulic mining is abandoned completely.

BIBLIOGRAPHY

GENERAL CALIFORNIA HISTORY

Bancroft, Hubert H. v. 23 *History of California 1848-1859*. San Francisco, The History Co., 1888.

Gudde, Erwin G. *California Place Names*. Berkeley and Los Angeles, University of California Press, 1969.

Rensch, H. E. and E. G.; and Hoover, Mildred. *Historic Spots in California*. Stanford, Stanford University Press, 1966. $10.00.

Rolli, Andrew F. *California: A History*. New York, Thomas Y. Crowell Company, 1969.

State of California, Department of Parks & Recreation, Division of Beaches and Parks. *California Historical Landmarks*. Sacramento, 1968. $1.00.

GOLD RUSH HISTORY

Automobile Club of Southern California. *Guide to the Mother Lode Country*, 1971. Paperback guidebook for members features towns found along State Highway 49 from Mariposa to Sattley.

Brockman, Christian Frank. *A Guide to the Mother Lode Country*. Yosemite Nature Notes, vol. 27, no. 1. Mariposa County Historical Society, 1948. Forty-eight page paperback tour of selected towns in the Gold Country.

Caughey, John W. *Gold Is the Cornerstone*. Berkeley, University of California Press, 1948. General analysis of the Gold Rush era.

Fairchild, Frances. *The Life and Times of Gen. John A. Sutter, and other Historical Sketches*. Sacramento, A. N. Bullock, 1913.

Gardiner, Howard C. *In Pursuit of the Golden Dream; Reminiscences of San Francisco and the Northern and Southern Mines, 1849-1857*. Stoughton, Mass., Western Hemisphere, Inc., 1970. California Gold Rush in retrospect. A "look backward" as seen through diaries and letters written en route or after reaching the gold mines. Explains origin of some camps' picturesque names.

Jackson, Joseph Henry. *Anybody's Gold: The Story of California's Mining Towns*. San Francisco, Chronicle Books, 1970. $7.95. Tells actual tales of gold-seekers. Makes Gold Country "come alive" from descriptions of its people.

Nadeau, Remi. *Ghost Towns and Mining Camps of California*. Los Angeles, The Ward Ritchie Press, 1965. $5.95.

Sargent, Shirley. *Mariposa County Guidebook*. Yosemite, Flying Spur Press, 1967. $1.00. Outline of seven historical tours in Mariposa County stressing little-known facts about the area.

Stellman, Louis J. *Mother Lode: The Story of California's Gold Rush*. San Francisco, Harr Wagner, 1934.

Sunset Books. *Ghost Towns of the West*. Menlo Park, Lane Magazine & Book Company, 1971. $11.75. What is a ghost town, where are they found, where did everybody go? This book answers these questions with facts and photographs.

MINING

May, Philip Ross. *Origins of Hydraulic Mining in California*. Oakland, The Holmes Book Co., 1970. $6.95. Concise history of hydraulic mining from its inception in 1853 to its demise in 1884.

Paul, Rodman W. *California Gold*. Cambridge, Harvard University Press, 1965. Basic modern work on principal techniques of mining.

Paul, Rodman W. (ed.) *The Miners' Own Book*. San Francisco, Book Club of California, 1949. Reprinted from the original edition of 1858. Illustrations and descriptions of various methods of California mining.

State of California, Dept. of Natural Resources, Division of Mines. *Geologic Guidebook Along Highway 49 — Sierran Gold Belt: The Mother Lode Country*. (Centennial Edition, Bulletin 141), 1948. Bible for geologists. Usually available only in reference libraries.

Wagner, Jack R. *Gold Mines of California*. Berkeley, Howell-North Books, 1970. $10.00. History of large-scale gold mining in the Mother Lode and Northern Mines. Includes many photographs, paintings, and sketches.

LIFE IN THE GOLD FIELDS

Buffum, E. Gould. *Six Months in the Gold Mines*. Los Angeles, The Ward Ritchie Press, 1958. $5.00. One of the earliest and most vivid accounts of the excitement, hardships, and rewards of placer mining.

Clappe, Louise. *The Shirley Letters from the California Mines 1851-1852*. New York, Alfred A. Knopf, 1961. $5.95. Paperback edition, $2.95. A woman's view of life in a gold camp.

Delano, Alonzo. *Life on the Plains and Among the Diggings*. Auburn, N.Y., 1854. One of the best of many contemporary accounts by a California gold-seeker.

Jackson, W. Tarrentine. *Twenty Years on the Pacific Slope*. New Haven and London, Yale University Press, 1965. $6.00. Letters of Henry Eno from California and Nevada 1848-1871. A first-hand report of the changing scene, not only during the Gold Rush period but after the peak of the excitement.

Perkins, William. *Three Years in California*. Berkeley, University of California Press, 1964. William Perkins' journal of life at Sonora, 1849-1852.

MISCELLANEOUS

Bristow, Gwen. *Calico Palace*. New York, Thomas Y. Crowell Company, 1970. Paperback edition, $1.25. Fictional account of life in San Francisco and the Sierra foothills during the Gold Rush.

Foley, Doris. *The Divine Eccentric*. Los Angeles, Westernlore Press, 1969. $7.50. Lola Montez, according to newspaper articles; also contains her autobiography.

Garbarini, Evelyn, as told by the late Emmet H. Garbarini. *The Kennedy Wheels*. Jackson, Amador Progress-News, 1967. $1.00. Story of the building of the large Kennedy tailing wheels in Amador County.

Lewis, Oscar. *Sea Routes to the Gold Fields*. New York, Alfred A. Knopf, Inc., 1949. How the argonauts reached California by ship.

Lewis, Oscar. *Sutter's Fort, Gateway to the Gold Fields*. Englewood Cliffs, N.J., Prentice-Hall, 1966. Paperback edition, $1.25.

Stegner, Wallace. *Angle of Repose*. New York, Doubleday & Company, Inc., 1970. $7.95. Fictitious novel, based on historical fact, of the West of mining days, the West of today, and the West in between.

Strong, Phil. *Gold In Them Hills*. New York, Doubleday & Company, Inc., 1957. $3.50. An "irreverent history of the great Gold Rush" — combination of actual historical fact with fictional characters.

GLOSSARY OF MINING TERMS

Argonauts — term used interchangeably with '49er to refer to first gold-seekers in California.

Assay office — a place that evaluated mineral content of ore by chemical analysis.

Bar — pertaining to banks of sand or gravel that extended into a river. Later used to describe any camp that sprang up alongside a river bar, such as Chili Bar.

Bullion — unminted gold or silver. Usually melted into bricks or bars for easy storage.

Claim — piece of land that was staked out by a miner for working.

Color — term usually used to indicate finding evidence of gold.

Diggings — early mining term referring to a claim that was being worked for gold.

Dust — minute particles of gold taken by placer mining and used as a form of money. In many camps $1 was the amount of "dust" that could be held between thumb and forefinger; also called "pinch."

Fandango hall — Mexican drinking and gambling halls. Named after the "fandango," a castanet-clacking dance.

Flume — inclined trough, usually built of wood, used to convey water for long distances.

Glory hole — holes from which unusually rich deposits of gold-bearing ore were extracted.

Going to see the elephant — phrase used by greenhorns to describe their anticipated experiences in the gold fields.

Gulch — deep, narrow valley or ravine. Because of their location, many mining camps contained the word "gulch" as part of their name.

Headframe — also known as gallows frame. Wooden structure erected over the top of a shaft used to raise and lower ore buckets.

Highgrade — gold-rich ore. A "highgrader" was someone who removed gold from a claim without obtaining authorization.

Hydraulicking — an effective but destructive method of mining. Water under pressure was directed at soft gravels, causing dirt to run down into sluice boxes and banks to disintegrate.

I.O.O.F. — a fraternal order to which large numbers of gold miners belonged. Also known as Odd Fellows.

Joss house — Chinese temple used as a place of worship. An excellent example is in Oroville.

Monitor — huge nozzle used to direct jets of water in hydraulic mining. Sometimes referred to as "giants."

Nugget — lump of gold of any size, usually larger than the head of a match. Largest found weighed 195 pounds.

Panning — a simple, but slow, method of mining. Gravels from stream bed are washed in pan, causing lighter materials to spill over side and heavier gold-bearing particles to settle to bottom.

Pay dirt — expression describing gold-rich ore taken from claims.

Pocket—a small concentration of gold-bearing gravel.

Poke — amount of gold dust or nuggets miner owned; usually carried in a crude leather pouch.

Quartz — mineral generally found in large masses or veins. The quartz in the Sierra Nevada was mined for its gold content.

Retort — furnace used to heat gold and mercury. Mercury was vaporized and gold left was formed into bars.

Rocker — wooden rectangular box set on rockers, used in mining. Rocking motion caused mixture of dirt and water to flow through box, with gold-bearing particles caught by riffles.

Sluice boxes—a modified rocker. Water power forced dirt through the box with gold-bearing particles caught by riffles.

Stamp mill — a mill built to break up and grind gold-bearing ore.

Strike — a new-found concentration of gold rich enough to be mined profitably.

Tailings — waste material left after gold-bearing ore was processed.

Vein — route followed by gold from lower depths toward surface.

Worked out—referring to an area from which all gold was thought to have been extracted.

INDEX

PHOTOGRAPHERS